The Lake Superior
Iron Ore Railroads

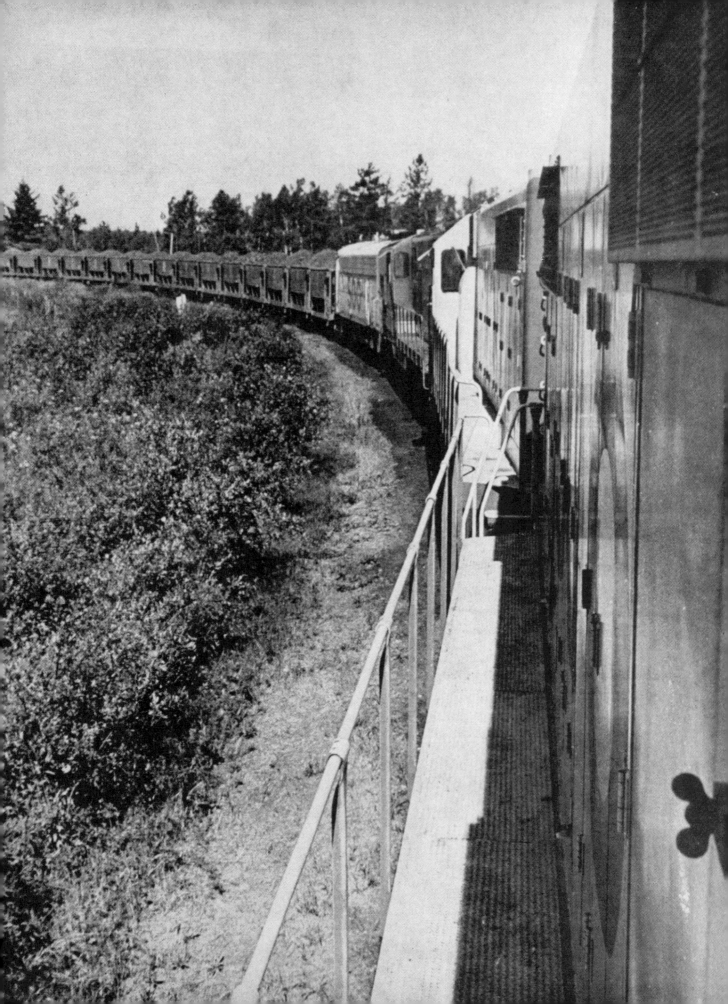

The
Lake Superior
Iron Ore Railroads

by

PATRICK C. DORIN

Bonanza Books • New York

Dedicated To

My wife, Karen and children
Thomas, Michael and Susan
who made many sacrifices and
gave encouragement during
the writing of this book.

CONTENTS

Foreword

THE PURPOSE of this book is to describe the iron ore hauling railroads of the Lake Superior Region. Few people outside the Lake Superior District have any idea about some of the heaviest, hardest railroading in the world. There are 11 ore haulers in Minnesota, Wisconsin, Michigan and Ontario, 9 are common carriers and two are private lines. Together, they presently handle in excess of 100 million tons annually of raw iron ore, raw taconite ore, taconite pellets, iron ore pellets, and various other types of iron ore products from mine and processing plant to the lake ports.

The iron ore lines have a romance all of their own. They operate in the land of the Northern Lights—the land of sky blue waters. They used the heaviest steam locomotives. They run the world's heaviest trains. They use the shortest freight equipment—24 feet long. Centralized Traffic Control is used extensively and the newest streamliner in the Mid-west can take you to the Ore Country.

The material in this book was gathered by this writer through interviews, field trips, let-ters of inquiry, various company files and personal employment on two of the ore railroads.

This writer would like to thank the officers, staff members and employees of the following companies, who gave their kind assistance in gathering materials and data for this book: The Duluth, Missabe and Iron Range Railway, The Lake Superior and Ishpeming Railroad, The Great Northern Railway, The Chicago and North Western Railway, The Milwaukee Road, The Soo Line Railroad, The Northern Pacific Railway, The Canadian National Railways, The Erie Mining Company, The Reserve Mining Company, The Union Pacific Railroad, The Southern Pacific Company, The Penn Central Railroad, Pickands Mather, Alco Products, Inc., ACF Industries, Bethlehem Steel Company, Greenville Steel Car, Pullman Standard, National Car, International Car, Thrall Manufacturing, General Electric and the United States Steel Corporation.

Patrick C. Dorin

Duluth, Minnesota

Chapter One

The "Why" Of It All

THE UNITED STATES and Canada, have a combined population of over 220 million people. These people use over 100 million tons of steel annually for just about every type of product on today's market. One does not have to look far to see a steel product or a product that was manufactured by steel.

Steel is made from iron, and iron is made from iron ore. Most of the steel mills are located in relation to the principal market areas. Therefore, iron ore is transported hundreds of miles to the mills.

The principal iron deposits are located in the Lake Superior District, Quebec-Labrador Region, Newfoundland and Alabama. There are also lesser deposits located in Pennsylvania, Missouri, Texas, Utah, Wyoming, California, British Columbia, Ontario and Mexico.

Each ore source has its own market area. The Lake Superior ores serve the Great Lakes Region steel mills. Quebec-Labrador ores are shipped to the Eastern Great Lakes Region Mills and to the Atlantic Coast Plants.

Of all the iron mining districts, the Lake Superior District is one of the greatest iron mining regions in the world, either on a basis of past production or future potential.

Iron ore was first discovered in the Lake Superior Region in 1844 near the city of Negaunee, Michigan on the Marquette Range. Ore was discovered on the Vermilion Range, Minnesota in 1865; the Menominee Range, Michigan in 1872; the Crystal Falls, Michigan, Florence, Wisconsin and Iron River, Michigan Districts in 1880; the Gogebic Range in 1882; the Great Mesabi in 1890; and the Cuyuna Range in Minnesota in 1903. The important Steep Rock, Ontario body was not discovered until 1938.

There are various types of ores in the Lake Superior Region. They vary widely in mineral-ogy and chemical composition and physical characteristics.

The ores include merchantable furnace ores and lump ores (soft and hard ores respectively), beneficiating ores (ores that can be easily beneficiated by gravity methods), magnetite taconite, jasper ores and semitaconite.

All ores shipped from the Lake Superior District are classified as either blast furnace ores or open hearth ores.

The blast furnace ores are commonly blended products from more than one mine, and sometimes represent a blend of natural ores, coarse or fine, and beneficiated products. The natural ores are shipped as either standard unscreened ore, or their coarse and fine screened fractions.

As mentioned above, the Lake Superior District's iron mining ranges are the Mesabi, Vermilion and the Cuyuna in Minnesota; the Gogebic, Menominee, and Marquette in Michigan and the Steep Rock in Ontario. At the present time, the Vermilion and the Gogebic are inactive and the Cuyuna is a very small producer.

The Mesabi Range is located about 70 miles north of Duluth. It consists of a belt of iron formation about 120 miles long with the town of Grand Rapids near the west end and Babbitt near the east end. Iron bearing rocks of the iron formation were known in the area in 1866, but commercial iron ore was not discovered until 1890. The colors of Mesabi ores are red, blue, yellow and brown.

The Vermilion Range is situated in the northeastern part of Minnesota about 75 miles north of Duluth and 55 miles from Lake Superior. The range is 22 miles long with Tower and Soudan on the west and Ely on the east. Ore was mined on the range from 1884 to April 1, 1967 when the Pioneer Mine was closed.

HEAVY STEAM SWITCHERS were used during the days of steam for working the mines. Here an 0-8-0 is shown switching a string of ore cars in the Mahoning Mine in 1937.—*Courtesy Great Northern Railway.*

The Cuyuna Range is located 100 miles west southwest of Duluth, and has a length of 68 miles. Mining, however, is confined to an area about 10 miles long near Crosby and Ironton.

The Marquette Range is located in the northern part of the Upper Peninsula of Michigan with its eastern end 10 miles west of the City of Marquette. It is about 30 miles long and 6 miles wide. The range includes the towns of Negaunee, Ishpeming, Palmer, Humboldt, Republic, and Michigamme. The major portion of of the ore has been mined by underground methods.

The ores of the Marquette Range include both hard lump open hearth and soft furnace ores.

The Menominee Range is located along the southern boundary of the Upper Peninsula in the vicinity of Iron Mountain and in the adjacent part of Northern Wisconsin. It has three active producing districts: Iron River, Crystal Falls, and Felch Mountain; and three inactive areas: Menominee and Amasa, Michigan and Florence, Wisconsin.

The Penokee-Gogebic Range, commonly known as the Gogebic, is located in Northern Wisconsin and the western end of the Upper Peninsula of Michigan. It is about 80 miles in length and strikes in an east-west direction with the towns of Mellen and Hurley, Wisconsin and Ironwood, Bessemer and Wakefield, Michigan. The high cost of underground mining has terminated operations of all the mines, and the deepest ore has not been exhausted.

IRON ORE from U.S. Steel's Sherman open pit mine on Minnesota's famed Mesabi Range is loaded by electric shovels into railroad cars for transportation to a beneficiation plant on the surface. The shovel loads 13 tons with each scoop. All of the ore mined in Minnesota today must be processed in one way or another before it is shipped to the steel mills. The Sherman, located at Chisholm, Minnesota, is one of the largest iron ore producers in the State.—*Courtesy U.S. Steel*

THE MINING COMPANIES used large steam switchers for working the mines. This locomotive was owned by Oliver Iron Mining Division of U.S. Steel. The locomotive had a booster on the front truck of the tender. With this booster, the locomotive had a total tractive effort of 69,500 pounds. The locomotive was built in 1927 by the Lima Locomotive Company.—*Courtesy W. C. Olsen*

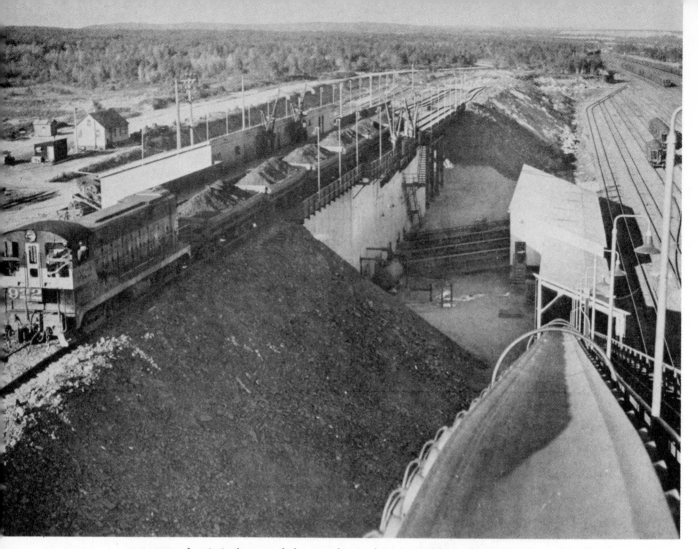

ALL ORE, after it is dug out of the ground, must be improved by washing, screening or by other mechanical or chemical methods. Here a U.S. Steel mine train is arriving at a dumping station at an Improvement Plant. After the ore has been processed, it will be loaded into ore cars in the yard at the right hand side of the photo.—*Courtesy W. C. Olsen.*

A GREAT DEAL of Minnesota ore is sent to the Lake Michigan Steel Centers. This photo shows the ore docks unloading iron ore from the *"Benjamin F. Fairless"* at the Gary Steel Works. One can see Elgin, Joliet & Eastern Railway hopper cars on the ore dock near the bow of the ship. Ore is loaded into cars on the dock for movement to the open hearths, which are located behind the blast furnaces and cannot be served directly by the ore docks.—*Courtesy U.S. Steel*

SHIPS ARE USED to carry ore and pellets from the Lakes Superior and Michigan ports to the steel producing centers. Here is an artist's rendition of a giant new Great Lakes vessel being built for moving taconite pellets. The ship will be 858 feet long and will have a 105 foot beam, making it 128 feet longer and 30 feet wider than any vessel now in service on the Great Lakes. At full draft design, it will be capable of transporting a cargo of 45,000 gross tons. The vessel will be operating to ports on Lakes Superior, Michigan, Huron and Erie.—*Courtesy U. S. Steel*

The future of this range depends upon the development of deposits of magnetite taconite located in the Wisconsin Section of the Range.

The Steep Rock Lake area is located three miles north of Atikokan, Ontario and 140 miles west of Lake Superior at Port Arthur.

Historically since the development of mining and steel making, the avenues of iron ore commerce have been rail and water. The great Lake Superior Iron Ore District has occupied a very strategic location with respect to water routes along the Great Lakes to the steel centers on Lake Erie and Lake Michigan and in the Pittsburgh and Youngstown areas. As much

as 96 million tons in one year have been shipped through the Great Lakes Ports in Minnesota, Wisconsin, Michigan and Ontario to the lower lake ports.

When the loaded ore vessels arrive at the lower lake ports, the ore is removed from the ships by Hulett electric unloaders or unloading rigs and transferred to stockpiles or to railroad cars of the Bessemer & Lake Erie, Penn Central, Erie-Lackawanna or others for shipment to inland mills.

Let's return to the North Country now, and take a close look at the transportation of iron ore by rail from mine to dock.

THE FINAL DESTINATION of iron ore is the ore storage yards of the steel mills. This yard is at the Duquesne Works of U. S. Steel.—*Courtesy U. S. Steel*

U. S. STEEL'S MINNTAC PLANT near Mountain Iron, Minnesota. Here facilities crush, grind and separate iron ore particles from tough iron-bearing taconite rock to produce 4.5 million tons of quality iron ore pellets annually. Minntac plant, and the mine which produces the crude taconite rock, operate year-round. On the right hand side is a DM&IR unit train being loaded with pellets.—*Courtesy U.S. Steel.*

ORE DESTINED to the Pittsburgh and Youngstown areas from the Lake Superior Region must be unloaded from the ships and loaded into railroad cars for movement to the inland mills. This operation is taking place at the Penn Central's ore dock at Cleveland, Ohio.—*Courtesy Penn Central*

THE CANADIAN NATIONAL and the Ontario Northland Railway operate daily unit trains of iron ore pellets from the Sherman mine at Temagami, Ontario to the steel mills at Hamilton, Ontario. This is the first such train to depart Temagami. Note the pine tree on the first carload of pellets. (It is the custom that whenever a new mine and/or pellet plant is opened, that a pine tree is placed on the first load.) Each unit train contains 35 cars. There are three trains operating on 72 hour cycles. — *Courtesy Ontario Northland Railway*

A CLOSE UP view of the new type of ore car being used in the Temagami-Hamilton, Ontario unit train service. This is the only covered hopper type of ore car being operated in the iron ore service.—*Courtesy Canadian National*

THE PENN CENTRAL, although it does not serve a major ore producing region, is a major ore hauler. In fact, it moves approximately 28 million tons per year, which is about 3 million tons more than the Duluth, Missabe & Iron Range Railway handles. The DM&IR is the largest common carrier ore hauler in the Lake Superior region.

The Penn Central, in addition to handling Lake Superior ore from Lake Erie ports, also handles a large amount of foreign iron ore. This photo shows the Penn Central's huge ore unloading facility on the Delaware River at Philadelphia handling two carriers at the same time. Ore from foreign fields is removed from the holds of the vessels by the huge machines and is transported by moving belts to the elevated building in the background where it is weighed and loaded into hopper cars moving in a steady pace through the facility. The ore is transported to inland steel mills. To the left of the elevated structure is shown a part of the huge storage pile of ore awaiting shipment. To the right and in the left distance are the yards in which empty cars are assembled and loaded units made up into trains. The skyline of Philadelphia is in the upper right.—*Courtesy Penn Central*

THERE ARE A NUMBER of railroads outside the Lake Superior Region that handle a substantial amount of iron ore or iron ore products. This photo shows a Union Pacific ore train, loaded with Wyoming Taconite Pellets, enroute to Utah steel mills.—*Courtesy Union Pacific*

THE FIRST UNIT train of iron ore pellets arriving at Hamilton, Ontario from Temagami.—*Courtesy Canadian National*

THE SOUTHERN PACIFIC Company hauls approximately 6.7 million tons of iron ore annually between Eagle Mountain, California and Kaiser Steel at Fontana, California; and to Long Beach, California for export. Here are three Southern Pacific units heading up a long ore train in CTC territory.
—*Courtesy Southern Pacific Company*

THIS ORE CAR looks like the type from Lake Superior Region. Except for the fact that it is slightly longer, it is identical to the DM&IR ore cars. Ore that rides the DM&IR often finds itself on the Bessemer and Lake Erie Railroad after its long lake voyage. The B&LE handles the ore to the Pittsburgh Mills from its lake port at Conneaut, Ohio.—*Courtesy Greenville Steel Car Co.*

HERE IS STILL ANOTHER example of a different shaped ore car. This car is used by the Quebec, North Shore and Labrador Railroad.—*Courtesy Pullman Standard*

OPERATING RULES for ore trains on the UP are similar to those in effect on the Lake Superior District roads. For example, the speed limit for trains, when 50% or more of the tonnage is ore, is 40 MPH. The Northern Pacific's speed limit for trains handling loaded ore cars is also 40 MPH.—*Courtesy Union Pacific*

A 100 TON ORE CAR built for the Southern Pacific Company by Thrall Car Manufacturing Company. The SP handles a substantial amount of iron ore and has a large fleet of ore cars for that traffic. Most of the SP's ore business is located in Southern California. Note the similarities between this ore car and the ones used in the Lake Superior Region. This car is also five feet longer.—*Courtesy Thrall Car. Mfg. Co.*

THE UNION PACIFIC has a large fleet of these 30 foot ore cars. These cars are used in taconite service in Wyoming and Utah.—*Courtesy Union Pacific Railroad Co.*

Chapter Two

Duluth, Missabe and Iron Range Railway

THE DULUTH, MISSABE and Iron Range Railway is truly one of the most remarkable railroads in the world. It has one of the best safety records. It carries a substantial tonnage, over 50 millions tons of all types of freight during a Korean War year, and now the usual tonnage is about 25 million tons per year. Many roads with similar mileage (the DM&IR has 560 route miles) carry only 5 to 6 million tons of freight per year. Most of the traffic on the DM&IR is ore, but other traffic consists of pulpwood, refrigerator blocks, coal, steel and so on in just about every type of car that can be found on the American Railroads.

Even though the DM&IR serves a considerable amount of bush country, it is no bush country railroad by any standard. It has heavy 115 pound to 132 pound rail in the main lines, double track from Duluth to the Mesabi Range with welded rail in the south bound main for the loaded ore trains, automatic block signals, centralized traffic control, radio equipped cabooses, motive power and stations, a fleet of immaculate SD-9's and SD-18's and nearly 12,000 pieces of freight equipment to move the customers' traffic. A good criterion of a railroad is the amount of freight equipment it owns, and the DM&IR has more equipment than some lines with 4,000 or more route miles.

The DM&IR operates left handed in their double track territory. This is contrary to the belief that the Chicago & North Western Railway is the only line to do so.

The DM&IR's main function is the transportation of iron ore to the ore docks at Duluth and Two Harbors. The railroad extends from those two ports to the Mesabi Range over three different lines. In addition, there is a line that extends east and west on the Range which connects all the lines running to the shores of Lake Superior.

The Missabe Road is divided into two divisions. The Missabe Division, which consists of the old Duluth, Missabe & Northern Railway; and the Iron Range Division, which consists of the old Duluth and Iron Range Rail Road. The two lines were consolidated in 1938. The operations of the two divisions are different because of the grades and the location of the docks to the ore dock yards. Hills have a very definite effect on railroad operations, and the DM&IR has their share of hills.

Ore is mined on the Mesabi in the DM&IR's territory. There is no mining anywhere on the Vermilion. Most of the ore comes from mines that lie in almost a straight line from Coleraine to Aurora, a distance of over 60 miles. This is the area of the east-west line mentioned above.

General Operating Procedures

In the morning of each day, all mining companies give the DM&IR an anticipated loading order for the following 24 hours. From this, the Yardmasters in charge can set up the switch crews for the next day. As the ore is loaded, orders are issued for the assembly of loads for the movement to Proctor or Two Harbors. The loads are assembled into trains at Coleraine, Wilpen, Fraser, Fayal, Aurora, Rainy Junction (Virginia), Biwabik and before the closing of the last mine on the Vermilion, Ely. At the present time, most of the ore trains are made up for Duluth. The year 1966 was the first in three that any ore was shipped through Two Harbors. Shipments had been down because of competition from foreign ores, the depletion of high grade natural ore deposits and the lack of a suitable tax structure, which

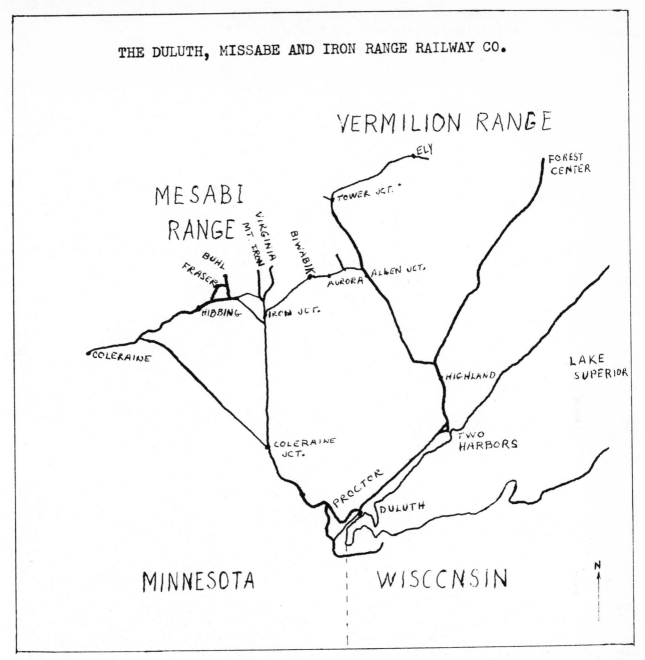

would have encouraged mining expansion. The latter was passed in the State of Minnesota in 1963, and the future is very bright for increased movement of ore, particularly in the form of processed taconite pellets.

In accordance with the mining requirements for cars, the mine run crews have the responsibility of distributing empties and assembling loads into road trains. Since 1966, the mine run crews have a new job to do: The hauling of raw taconite to the taconite pellet plants. After the taconite is processed into pellets, they are loaded into cars with 20 inch extensions. The pellets are usually loaded by the Road Crews in a Unit Train Operation.

When trains of ore have been assembled, the Chief Dispatcher at Iron Junction (The Operations Control Center for both Divisions) is notified and an ore extra is called out of Proctor or Two Harbors. This writer will cover each division and its dock operations separately.

The Missabe Division

The Missabe Division could truly be called one of the busier railroad divisions in the United States—excluding any commuter train operations. Anywhere from 12 to 18 ore extras per day roll over the Missabe Division, not to mention the mine run transfers, the Coleraine Local, the Rainy Jct. local and taconite unit trains to the Eveleth and Minntac Plants. (As time goes on, the number of taconite unit trains will increase while the number of raw iron ore trains will decrease.) The tonnage is immense. Let's take a look at how an ore extra is handled on the DM&IR's Missable Division.

The Missabe Division ore trains run from Proctor to any of the North End points mentioned above, such as Biwabik. The Chief Dispatcher is notified that a train of 180 to 200 loads will be ready at a North End point at a given time. In the meantime, he is also notified that a full train of 190 to 200 empties is ready at the Proctor Classification Yard. The Dispatcher then issues orders to run a road extra out of Proctor with the empties to a particular North End point and return with the loads. The train of empties was made up by the yard crews at Proctor and the caboose placed on the rear end.

The trip north consumes from 2 to 4 hours depending upon destination and delays. Upon arrival at the North End destination, the yardmaster notifies the crew what track the empties should be set out on. The yard crew then will distribute the empties to the various mines. The road crew couples on to the loaded train, eats lunch while the air is pumped up in the train, and begins the trip back to Proctor.

Upon arrival at the extreme west end of Proctor Yard, the train is cut in two for weighing. The road crew weighs the first half of the train, while a yard crew weighs the second half of the train.

It is here, at the entrance to Proctor Yard, that one of the most unique operations in America comes into play. The DM&IR has pioneered in the development of an Automatic Car Identification System in its practical application. This system reads and records car numbers by the means of the energy of light.

As the cars are weighed, the ACI scanner reads and records the car numbers and light weight from a color coded panel on the side of the car. This information is input for a computer which makes a subtraction to give ore weight, and relays the information to a teleprinter tape puncher. The weighmaster then transmits the data to the yard, dock office, Iron Junction Operations Center and the Mining Companies by running the tape through the teleprinter.

The road engine proceeds through the scale with the first half of the train. The weighing is done at the rate of about 5 to 6 cars per minute.

After the road crew has completed their responsibility, the cut is yarded and engine crew returns to the roundhouse, their part of the job of transporting the iron ore completed.

The next phase in the transportation of Missabe Division ore from mine to dock is the Proctor Yard Classification. Proctor Yard is one of the largest yards in the Upper Mid-west. It has 75 miles of track and a storage capacity of 3,000 cars. Classification of the ore is performed at this yard, which serves the Duluth ore docks. All switching power and cabooses are equipped with radios for fast communication between the yard office and other crews. For night operation, the entire yard is illuminated by mercury vapor floodlights.

After the ore has been classified, it remains in Proctor Yard until called for by the Ore Dock Office. When this occurs, the loads specified for a certain boat load are collected into 100 to 117 car trains. These trains are called the Hill Ore Trains because of the Steep Hill between Proctor and the Ore Docks. The steepest part of the grade is 2.18%. The train is assembled by the Hill Crew and a caboose is placed on the rear. All the retainers are set before the train leaves the yard for the docks. As the train rolls down the hill, the speed must be limited to 25 MPH for the seven mile trip.

Just before the train arrives at the approaches to the ore docks, Collingwood to be exact, the caboose is cut off the train on the fly. The train rolls out on to the approaches, with the dynamic brake cooling fans screaming, and the brakes shoes on the ore cars giving off a blue smoke. The train stops just before the dock itself with the grace of a passenger train.

The DM&IR has two steel and concrete docks of identical length in Duluth. The docks are 2,304 feet long and have 384 pockets, 192 to a side. Dock No. 5 will hold four 70 ton cars of ore per pocket, while No. 6 will hold 5 cars of ore per pocket. No. 5's capacity is 115,200 tons and No. 6 is 153,600 tons. The Duluth docks hold a 24 hour loading record. On June 7, 1944, 35 vessels were loaded with 406,269 tons of ore.

When the ore arrives at the Duluth Docks, or any railroad's docks for that matter, a host of problems are facing all the employees. It might appear to be rather simple to unload the cars and transfer the ore into boats upon their arrival. The mines produce a wide variety of grades of ore necessary to produce specific types of steel at the mills. Proctor Yard has the job of sorting this ore as mentioned above. This classification consists of more than types of ore, but selection of the best free running ores to assure best dispatch of vessels; and also to assure that each pocket will be kept chemically on grade to maintain quality control for best utilization in the blast furnaces and open hearths.

With these problems also come the problems of switching and car dumping with certain types of fine ores. Most of the difficulty in handling fines is caused by its highly cohesive characteristics. In order to minimize this problem, a coarse ore is usually dumped into the pocket first. Also a pattern of dumping is followed by dumping the first three cars from the inside track and the last one or two on the outside track. Ore dumped from the inside track has a tendency to reduce the compactness of the ore in the pocket, thereby permitting the ore to flow more easily into a vessel. This operation requires additional switching and restricts effective utilizaton of dock capacty. As the percentage of pellets increases over the next few years, the above problems of switching and unloading the cars will decrease.

In this Northland, cold weather can be expected in April, November and December during the shipping season. When this happens, the ore freezes in the cars enroute from the mines and freezes in the docks. In the past, before diesels, steam power was used to thaw the ore in the cars and in the docks for the loading of ships. Dieselization has eliminated the steam locomotive, and it is too costly to maintain such power for use only a few weeks out of every year. Therefore, the No. 5 ore dock has been equipped with a portable 36 car, gas-fired, under the car type of heating plant. The gas fired burners are mounted between the rails to provide heat to thaw the frozen ore in the cars. Shields are put up to protect the thawing plant from the wind. When the dock engine switches this installation, the crew must push the cars in or pull out very slowly, and an empty car is used for reaching into the thawing plant to couple or uncouple the loads.

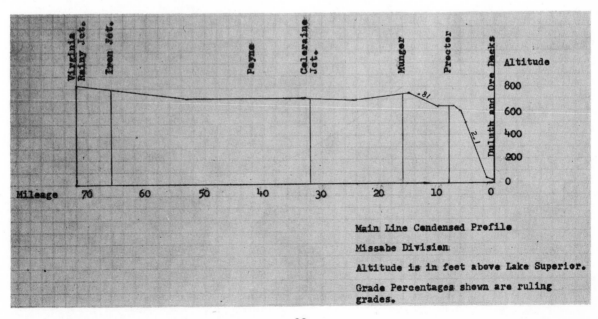

Main Line Condensed Profile

Missabe Division

Altitude is in feet above Lake Superior.

Grade Percentages shown are ruling grades.

23

Not infrequently, once the ore has been thawed in the ore car and dumped into the dock pocket, it freezes before being loaded into the ore vessel. The DM&IR has developed a new Boiler Car for use in washing the ore out of the pocket, called slushing service. The car is a converted locomotive tender from a retired Class E-4 steam locomotive (2-10-4). The requirements for slushing are that the equipment must be mobile and furnish at least 5,100 gallons per hour of hot water at a temperature of 180°. The boiler cars are equipped as follows: a 17,200 gallon water compartment, 1,400 gallon fuel oil storage tank, water softener, water supply pump, tank water level indicator gauge, injectors, each with 3,800 gallons per hour capacity, hose reels, steam boiler, 25 KW diesel electrical generating plant, 250 gallon boiler feedwater tank with float valve, chemical feeder pump, 24 gallon per hour compound treatment tank and electrical switch gear. These cars are used on both the Two Harbors and Duluth docks. They are placed on top of the ore dock and the hoses are placed into the pockets. As the hot water runs into the pocket, the ore thaws and flows into the ore boat. The thawing of frozen ore has always been a costly and difficult job for the railroads in trying to extend the shipping season.

Missabe Division Taconite Operations

Taconite pellets have brought a new era to the DM&IR ore docks n Duluth. To handle this new traffic—and on a year around basis —the East Side of the No. 6 ore dock has been modified along with the building of a storage area 800 feet wide and 1800 feet long. The storage area has a capacity of 2¼ million tons. During the winter, the production of the taconite plants is moved to the docks by unit ore trains, unloaded in the modified pockets and transferred to stockpile by the conveyor system. Pellets are loaded out of stockpile during the shipping season by a special bucket wheel reclaimer, moved to the top of the dock by conveyor system and deposited into the pockets for gravity loading into ore carriers. During the shipping season, pellets are handled directly through the ore docks in the usual manner. The capacity of each pocket on the No. 6 ore dock is 300 tons of pellets. Sinter and nodules are other iron ore products handled at the storage facility. At the present time (1968), the Missabe Road is handling approximately 5 million tons of taconite pellets per year. Additional plants and mines are also in the planning stage that will be using the DM&IR's transportation facilities, which means that the Missabe Division has a very sound future ahead of it.

The Iron Range Divison

The Iron Range Division Main Line extends northward between Two Harbors and the Vermilion Range, with a branch extending west from Allen Junction serving the eastern end of the Mesabi Range. In the past, the bulk of the ore mined in these areas was moved to Two Harbors. However, at the time of this writing, only ore or agglomerates that cannot be moved efficiently through Duluth, moves through Two Harbors. Approximately 2½ million tons of ore moved through the Two Harbors docks in 1966.

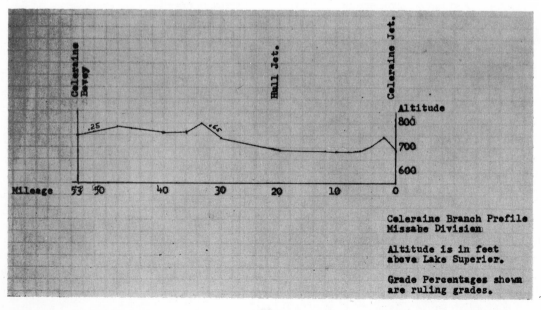

Coleraine Branch Profile
Missabe Division

Altitude is in feet above Lake Superior.

Grade Percentages shown are ruling grades.

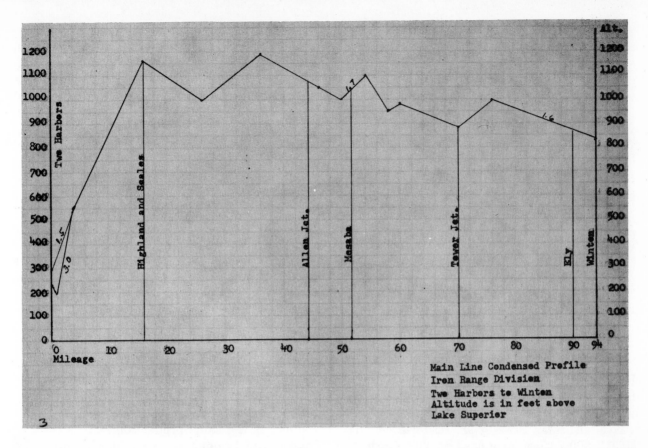

Main Line Condensed Profile
Iron Range Division
Two Harbors to Winton
Altitude is in feet above
Lake Superior

The docks were closed from 1962 through 1965. In years past, Two Harbors shipped as much as 19 million tons in a shipping season. Their 24 hour loading record is 17 boats, 198,040 tons on June 7, 1944.

There are 3 concrete and steel ore docks. The No. 1 is 1344 feet long, 75 feet high and has a capacity of 56,000 tons. No. 2 is 1368 feet long, 80 feet high and has a capacity of 68,400 tons. The No. 6 is 888 feet long, 74 feet high and has a capacity of 44,400 tons. The No. 6 ore dock is the smallest on the Great Lakes and presently is not being used. It is interesting to note that the DM&IR's No. 6 ore dock in Duluth is the largest in the world. The No. 1 ore dock in Two Harbors is the fastest loading dock on the Great Lakes.

A tug boat, the "Edna G," is maintained by the DM&IR to assist incoming boats to the docks; and to assist boats in departing Two Harbors.

The ore docks can be viewed very nicely from a Lake Front Park that has been provided through the courtesy of the DM&IR. It is very unusual to find a company providing parks for the general public, but the DM&IR leaves nothing unturned in promoting and maintaining a good public image.

The mine loading procedures are exactly the same as described in the section on the Missabe Division. In many respects, the Iron Range Division is identical to its sister division, but in many ways not. The mine run transfers operate exactly the same way. The road ore trains are assembled at Rainy Junction, Fayal, Biwabik and Aurora. Ore is not classified at any of these points. The differences between divisions occur in the road operations and dock operations.

Road trains originate at Two Harbors Yard and run to one of the above mentioned points. Trains are as long as 150 cars and are pulled by 3 SD-9's. At the present time, most of the ore is handled by the Ely and Rainy Junction Locals. Ore extras are called as they are needed. The ore is weighed in motion on automatic tract scales at Highland. After weighing, the trains roll for about 10 miles on a 1.5% descending grade to Waldo. The remaining distance of four miles to Two Harbors is at a descending grade of 3%. Two Harbors yard has a total of 177 tracks and over 60 miles of track.

From the yard, the cars are either sent directly to the dock if the block is in order for dumping, or the classification yard for sorting and storing in accordance with ore block requirements.

AN ENGINEER'S VIEW from an ore extra's locomotive of the Biwabik yard tower, a mine run assignment on the left and a cross country assignment.

When the ore dock office orders a specific block, a yard crew picks up the required cars and shoves them onto the dock over the designated pockets. Power used is a single unit locomotive, either an SD-9 or an SD-18. Alco 2400 HP DL-600's were once used at Two Harbors, but were recently sold to the Bessemer and Lake Erie.

When Two Harbors feels the cold pinch of winter and the ore freezes in the ore cars, the DM&IR has an excellent weapon, an Infrared Plant. Infrared rays, often called heat rays, are dependent upon radiation alone and not upon air circulation. Therefore, wind or low temper-

atures do not interfere with the effectiveness of this heat transmission.

The plant has a capacity of 36 cars. Since it is a far more rapid thawing operation, the plant has the same production rate as the former steam locomotive operation, in which 270 cars could be steamed simultaneously. In addition, infrared heating permits full tonnage loading in the ore cars which was not permissible with steaming. Thawing is quite rapid with the infrared plant. If there is a four inch frost depth, thawing requires only 23 minutes of heating time within the plant. Therefore, close communication must be maintained by

MINE TRAINS are fairly short and are usually powered by one unit. This one has just left the Biwabik yard and has 42 empties for a mine close by.

A DM&IR ORE TRAIN enroute to Proctor from Biwabik with 183 loads.

the Infrared Plant operator and the Yard Office and Ore Dock Office at all times to insure best possible dispatch of loads moving into and out of the plant.

Although the present tonnage through Two Harbors is very small, optimism among the residents of the Agate Bay City prevails regarding the future of Two Harbors as a port. Pellet production on the Mesabi Range is increasing year after year. It is felt that Duluth will not be able to handle all the pellets and other iron ore products that will soon be produced on the Mesabi. Therefore, it is hoped, the operations at Two Harbors, along with the col-

orful tug, the "Edna G", will be around for a long time to come.

Other Ore Operations

The DM&IR does a considerable amount of interchanging of ore with the Soo Line, Northern Pacific and the Great Northern. Ore from those lines is used for mixing on the Duluth docks, and ore goes to those lines for mixing on their docks.

The DM&IR serves the Duluth Works of the United States Steel Corporation and moves several thousand car loads of ore per year to that plant.

Each year, a certain amount of ore travels

IT IS A CLOUD of dust as ore trains meet on the double track line between Proctor and Iron Junction.

an all rail route to either the Chicago or St. Louis area steel mills. Whole trains of ore are delivered to the Chicago and North Western at Itasca (the C & NW uses 3 or 4 SD-40's for the all rail ore trains to Chicago or St. Louis), or the Soo Line at Ambridge. Usually trains of 100 cars are turned over to these two railroads for movement to the Steel Producing Centers.

This, then, is the story of how 1,700 employees use 80 locomotives and 9400 ore cars to move over 22 million tons of iron ore, pellets and other iron ore products to our Nation's Steel Mills, which in turn means so much to our economy and defense. A good job, well done by the Duluth, Missabe and Iron Range Railway.

THE WEST END of the Proctor Classification Yard. The SD-9 is pulling a string of loads from the arrival yard to the classification yard.

THE DM&IR could have claimed that it had the largest steam locomotive in the world in terms of tractive effort. The 2-8-8-4's, as shown here with the train leaving Virgina, had a tractive effort of 140,000 pounds. The Union Pacific Big Boy 4-8-8-4 weighed more than the DM&IR's Mallets, but their tractive effort was less than 130,000 pounds.—*Courtesy Wayne C. Olsen*

IN THE DAYS of steam, as now, the road crews on the DM&IR weighed the first half of their train upon arrival at Proctor. Here two 2-8-8-4's are rolling through the scales at the same time. In the background, one can see the arrival yard on the left and the departure yard on the right.—*Courtesy Wayne C. Olsen*

DURING THE DAYS OF STEAM, the DM&IR used 0-8-0's and 0-10-2's for switching the ore docks. This photo shows an 0-8-0 preparing to shove a train on to the No. 5 ore dock in Duluth. The train recently arrived from Proctor. Today, single unit SD-9's are used for dock service.—*Courtesy W. C. Olsen.*

THIS IS the striping that is read by the electronic scanner for the Automatic Car Identification System used by the DM&IR.

IN THE DAYS of steam, the DM&IR used 2-8-8-4's on most of their road trains. Here, Extra 232 South is rolling through Coleraine Junction, enroute to Proctor.—*Courtesy Wayne C. Olsen.*

SCENE AT DULUTH DOCK. Two vessels loading at No. 5 dock at Duluth.—*Courtesy DM&IR*

HERE IS A VIEW of the No. 6 ore dock at Duluth during the days of steam. The east side of the dock has been modified with a conveyor system to and from an outside taconite pellet storage facility. The locomotive on the dock is a 2-8-8-2 and it is preparing to leave for the Proctor classification yard.—*Courtesy W. C. Olsen*

HERE IS A VIEW of the Duluth ore docks during the time (1930) the last timber ore dock was being dismantled. Today, only the No. 5 (to the right) and the No. 6 remain. However, these docks are very efficient and can load over 25,000 tons into a vessel in about two hours. As yet, there are no conveyor loading systems on either the Great Lakes or the St. Lawrence River that can achieve this speed in loading ships.—*Courtesy W. C. Olsen*

AT ONE TIME, the Duluth, Missabe & Northern (now the Missabe Division of the DM&IR) operated four ore docks in Duluth. This photo was taken in the early 1900's when the motive power and the ore cars were small. Notice the short train in the left side of the photo enroute to Proctor. Later 2-8-8-2's handled about 80 cars up the hill, and now 2 SD-9's can handle about 120 cars.—*Courtesy Wayne C. Olsen*

THESE ARE NO. 1 AND NO. 2 ORE DOCKS in Duluth in the 1890's. Note the smaller steam locomotives and the wooden ore cars. There were many differences in the ships in those days too. Notice the whale back at the dock on the right hand side.—*Courtsy Wayne C. Olsen*

THIS VIEW shows how piping was connected to the steamers for steaming ore. Notice the upright pipe connected to the locomotive in the left side of the photo. The steam then flowed through pipes to the ore cars. On the right hand side, one can see the pipes attached to the steaming holes on the ore car. After the ore was thawed, it was a rush to get the cars down to docks in Duluth. This scene is in Proctor.—*Courtesy Wayne C. Olsen*

THIS MAN is inserting a steam pipe into a steaming hole on the side of the ore car. The men worked on 12 hour shifts on this very frantic job. There was never enough labor to handle this work.—*Courtesy Wayne C. Olsen*

DURING THE LATE FALL and early spring, the iron ore freezes in the ore cars. When it does, it must be thawed before it can be dumped into the ore dock. Steam power was used for this purpose. This scene shows such action at Proctor in the early 1940's. —*Courtesy Wayne C. Olsen*

STEAMING OPERATIONS at Proctor.—*Courtesy DM&IR*

ENGINE 229 moving to steaming plant at Two Harbors.—*Photo courtesy DM&IR*

HILL ORE TRAIN coming off Proctor steaming plant.—*Photo courtesy DM&IR*

THE DM&IR's Lakehead taconite pellet storage area. Pellets are emptied from the cars on the ore dock, and then transported by conveyor belt from the dock to stockpile. During the shipping season, the stockpiled pellets are taken back to the ore dock by conveyor belt and deposited into the dock pockets.

A TACONITE UNIT TRAIN leaving the No. 6 ore dock in Duluth.

THE TRAIN is now completely off the ore dock and the approaches and is moving up grade to Proctor at about 6 MPH.

THIS TRAIN will roll directly to a taconite plant on the Mesabi Range. Before 1966, ore trains did not normally run during the winter months. Now, with the taconite plants, and lake port storage facilities, ore trains carrying pellets roll all winter long.

THE TRAIN is rolling a little faster now as it goes by the 40th Ave. West crossing.

THE DM&IR has rebuilt many of their ore cars for taconite pellet service. The cars receive an 18 inch extension. Without such an extension, the ore cars as built, would not be able to carry 75 tons of pellets.

Next Page, **EXTRA 236 WEST** departing Two Harbors.—*Photo courtesy Frank King*

THE EXTENDED VISION cupola caboose was first purchased by the DM&IR in 1953. This type of caboose is widely recognized by safety people in the railroad industry as being about the best type of caboose on the market today.—*Courtesy International Car Corp.*

A UNIQUE SAFETY FEATURE, air brake hoses on DM&IR ore cars are shoulder level so that train crews do not have to bend down to couple hoses. When these cars are coupled to standard equipment, extension hoses must be used.—*Courtesy Pullman-Standard*

THIS IS THE ORE classification yard that serves the Number 1 and Number 2 ore docks at Two Harbors.

AT THE TIME of this writing (1968) most of the ore shipped through Two Harbors arrives in local freight trains. The DM&IR uses cabooses on both ends of way freights. This view shows the head-end of such a train after its arrival at Two Harbors.

THIS PHOTO shows an SD-9 getting a train ready for a shove onto the No. 2 ore dock. The long building in the background is the infrared plant at Two Harbors.

THE SD-9 is now shoving the train onto the No. 2 ore dock.

THIS VIEW shows the empty track that the train will arrive on. All ore docks on the Great Lakes have four tracks on top for dumping ore. Each pair of tracks serves the pockets for each side of the ore dock.

THE TRAIN has arrived on the dock, and the engineer will now be guided by both radio and hand signals for spotting the ore cars over the appropriate pockets. The crew will then gather up any empties that may be on the dock and return to the yard.

THE DM&IR maintains three ore docks at Two Harbors. Here is a view of the No. 1 ore dock with a loaded ore vessel getting ready to depart.—*Courtesy Wayne C. Olsen*

IN THIS SCENE, the tug *Edna G* has arrived to assist the ship in leaving the No. 1 ore dock.— *Courtesy Wayne C. Olsen*

A FEW MINUTES LATER, the ship has backed away from the ore dock, and the tug boat is turning the loaded vessel toward the entrance to the Two Harbors harbor.—*Courtesy Wayne C. Olsen*

THE CREW of the tug does not have any time to rest after assisting the *Swell Avery* out of the harbor. A few minutes later the *Williams*, another U.S. Steel vessel, requires assistance for docking. The ore dock in the background is the No. 2.—*Courtesy Wayne C. Olsen*

HERE IS A VIEW of the No. 2 ore dock loading the *Benjamin F. Fairless*. The ore cars on top of the ore dock will be unloaded directly into the ore boat through the pockets on the dock. These carloads are being used to top off the shipment of ore. The reason for this will be explained in detail in the chapter on Lake Superior & Ishpeming Railroad.—*Courtesy Wayne C. Olsen*

THIS PHOTO shows the No. 6 ore dock under construction at Two Harbors.—*Courtesy Wayne C. Olsen*

THE GARY loading at the No. 2 ore dock at night at Two Harbors.—*Photo Courtesy DM&IR.*

A NIGHT SCENE at Two Harbors.—*Courtesy DM&IR*

THIS VIEW shows the steaming of ore at Two Harbors. Now this has been replaced by an infrared plant. This photo shows the yards fairly well. On the right is the departure yard. The No. 6 ore dock is to the right also. The classification yards are in the center and to the left. The arrival yard is to the left of this photo.—*Courtesy Wayne C. Olsen*

THIS LOCOMOTIVE was originally owned by the Elgin, Joliet and Eastern Railway. Upon DM&IR dieselization in 1960, the engine was resold to the "J." The locomotive is now on display at Gateway Park—East Fourth Avenue in Gary, Indiana. This photo was taken at East Joliet yard.—*Courtesy EJ&E Railway.*

ON RARE OCCASIONS, a passenger extra rolls over the DM&IR. This one is a Director's Special and is shown here arriving at Endion (East Duluth yard) in the early evening.

Chapter Three

The Lake Superior and Ishpeming Railroad

THE LAKE SUPERIOR and Ishpeming Railroad serves the Marquette Iron Range in Northern Michigan. The railroad was built in 1896 and originated from a company known as the Plank Road. This Company hauled iron ore in 4 wheeled cars of three ton capacity, which were pulled by mules. Seventy-five per cent of the common stock of the LS&I is owned by Cleveland Cliffs Iron Company, the Road's major customer. The Railroad serves two counties, Marquette and Alger, and iron ore moves over nearly all LS&I trackage. The Road operates over 105 miles of main line track between Munising and Republic Mine with two branches from Lawson to Little Lake and from Stillman to Hartho. There is no iron ore traffic between Munising and Stillman. Munising is a very important source of paper traffic from the Kimberly-Clark Mills.

The principal part of the Railroad is that part from Marquette to Republic Mine. It is this section that has most of the traffic, and includes some of the most up to date railroading found anywhere in the world. This section of the Company carries over 5.5 million tons of raw ore and pellets per year. The LS&I is the fourth largest ore hauler in the Lake Superior District.

In order to handle this tonnage, the LS&I owns 19 diesel electric locomotives and over 3,000 pieces of rolling stock. The road owns 2,500 ore cars in the 50 ton, 70 ton, and 90 ton categories. The Road maintains yards for ore traffic at Humboldt, Ishpeming, Harris Yard (Negaunee), Eagle Mills (ore train assembly yard) and Marquette. At Marquette, the LS&I has a 1,200 foot ore dock with a 50,000 ton capacity.

The LS&I's operations can be split into four categories: The Mine Run Transfers, the Road Operations between Eagle Mills and the Ore Dock, the Ore Dock operations and the all rail ore movement to Eben and Little Lake. All four of these operations have a flavor all their own but are related to one another.

Mine Transfer Runs

Between Eagle Mills and Republic Mine, a distance of about 30 miles, the LS&I operates their mine transfer runs. The entire district is yard limits, which means the trains and engines do not have to comply with the flagging rule (Rule 99) unless they have occupied outfit cars in the train; and they must comply with Rule 93, which states they must run at restricted speed unless main track is seen or known to be clear. If the way is known to be clear, the trains may run at 20 MPH for the loaded trains and 25 MPH for the empties.

There are four yards in the Eagle Mills-Republic Mine District. The Eagle Mills Yard is used for the distribution of empties to mines and road train assembly. Harris Yard at Negaunee is used for overflow for empty ore cars —if Eagle Mills Yard cannot handle them. Euclid Yard at Ishpeming is used for interchanging ore with the Chicago & North Western Railway. Humboldt Yard is used for handling the switching at the Humboldt and Republic Mines.

The line west from Eagle Mills is quite interesting from a railroader's view point. The line consists of joint trackage with the Soo Line and C&NW and Centralized Traffic Control between Harris Yard and West Ishpening. The line may have any number of train and engine movements between Eagle Mills and Euclid Yard at Ishpeming, in fact up to 40 during a 24 hour period. In addition, there are at least 6 C&NW trains and 4 to 12 Soo Line train or engine movements daily in the CTC territory.

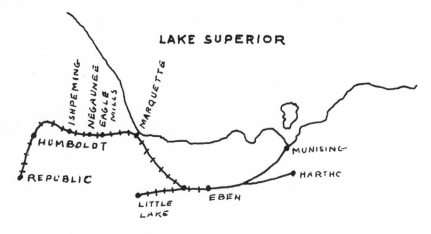

LAKE SUPERIOR

LEGEND

Not To Scale

+++ Ore Territory

—— Other LS&I Lines

The Eagle Mills Yard Office is the Operating Head Quarters for the Mine Run District. It has control over all yard assignments out of Eagle Mills for the Empire Mine, Pioneer Improvement Plant, Eagle Mills Pellet Plant, the Mather B Mine, Tilden Mine and runs east to Humboldt and beyond. It also has control over the Republic-Humboldt Mine assignment. This latter assignment is at the two mines at all times.

There are approximately 2 to 6 assignments per shift under control of the Eagle Mills Yardmaster. During the winter season, there are usually only 2 assignments per shift with one or none during the third trick. This depends upon the amount of all rail ore, the amount of raw ore moving to the Pioneer Improvement Plant from the Mather B Mine, and concentrate moving to the Pioneer and Eagle Mills Pellet Plants from Humboldt and Republic.

A typical switching assignment out of Eagle Mills looks something like this. Let's take a look at a 3 PM assignment going west to Humboldt. The crew picks up their locomotive at the Eagle Mills engine house. The power is usually two 1600 HP Alcos. The first assignment would be to go to the Eagle Mills Pellet Plant and pick up 40 empties of 154,000 pound capacity cars without extensions for concentrate hauling. They would then head west,

enter CTC territory and joint trackage with the Soo and C&NW and go directly to the Euclid Yard at Ishpeming. At that point, they would pick up about 100 empties from a C&NW ore train from Escanaba. (The LS&I does all C&NW ore switching on the Marquette Range.) After the crew has picked up the C&NW empties, the signal at the west end of the yard should show a red over green indication. This means a clear diverging route and that the switch is lined for the LS&I to leave the joint main line and travel their own line to Humboldt. The run to Humboldt may take up to two hours depending upon delays. Also, train speed can sometimes be as low as 5 or 6 MPH because of the grades of 1.5%. Some trains have stalled on these grades west of Ishpeming.

Upon arrival at Humboldt, the loaded train is usually made up by the switch engine stationed there. If it is not, the Eagle Mills engine drops its train on the main line and proceeds to make up its own train. The train consist eastbound varies between 70 and 125 cars. On one Saturday afternoon, this writer observed a train of 102 loads broken down as follows: 32 loads of pellets for the C&NW, 37 loads of concentrate for the Eagle Mills Pellet Plant and 33 cars of pellets for the ore dock at Marquette. (Concentrate is a processed ore but not yet pelletized.)

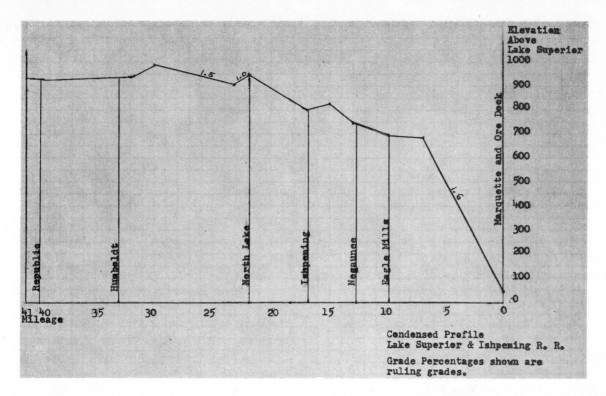

When the train is made up at Humboldt, the crew usually eats lunch and waits for the 5 p.m. yard assignment from Eagle Mills to arrive at Humboldt. Upon the arrival of the 5 p.m. assignment, the crew departs Humboldt and it may take about two hours before they reach Euclid Yard to set out the C&NW loads. After the Euclid Yard stop, the train then continues west climbing a very stiff grade toward Negaunee. Some of the trains require a helper engine out of Ishpeming to make the grade that begins just east of the depot. The automatic block signals east of Ishpeming have a permissive marker. This means that if the block signal is red, the trains may proceed at restricted speed without stopping. If the heavy trains were to stop on the hill, they would never start moving forward again.

Upon arrival at Eagle Mills, the crew would set out the cars for the ore dock and then continue on to the Eagle Mills Pellet Plant with the concentrate. When the concentrate is delivered, the crew returns to the engine house and their work is completed. This particular assignment takes anywhere from 7 to 12 hours to handle. Other yard assignments, other trains, snow, hot journals, any number of things can happen that will throw a crew's eight hour day off.

Other Eagle Mill assignments switch the various mines, the pellet plants, other industries and make up ore trains for Marquette. If

it is winter, the Eagle Mill crews may also assemble the all rail ore trains for the Soo at Eben and the C&NW at Little Lake. The assembled road ore train is the last phase in the Eagle Mills operation in the movement of ore from mine to dock.

The Road Operations

The LS&I has two main types of road operations in their ore hauling. The first is the hauling of the ore from Eagle Mills to Marquette and the ore dock. The second is the all rail ore movement to the connections at Eben and Little Lake. The LS&I also handles a certain amount of all rail ore in local trains for those points.

The LS&I has the shortest road movement from the mines to dock of any of the Lake Superior District railroads. The distance between Marquette and Eagle Mills is only 10 miles. Because of the short distance, the ore train crews make two round trips between Marquette and Eagle Mills instead of one as on the other railroad's ore train assignments. It takes about four hours for a round trip between Marquette and Eagle Mills, including time for lunch between runs.

These ore trains are known as the Hill Ore Trains because it is up grade all the way to Eagle Mills. The ruling grade is 1.6%. Ore trains run about 110 cars in both directions. Since the entire distance between Eagle Mills and Marquette is so short, the entire distance is operated as an absolute block and only one train is permitted in the single track territory at a time. Meets occur only at Marquette yard or at Eagle Mills and not in between.

In order to handle the 5½ million tons of ore annually over the ore dock, the LS&I usually runs about 3 crews per day over the main line. This means then that there are six loaded trains arriving at the Marquette ore yard nearly every day during the ore season. With the corresponding empty movements, one can expect to see 12 trains per day between Marquette and Eagle Mills. If the ore dock is loaded to near capacity awaiting the arrival of ore vessels, the crews may be cut to two for four loaded trains during that day. Often if there is a rush of boats, there may be four crews called during a day for a total of 8 loaded trains into the ore yard. Let's take a look at a typical ore train assignment between Marquette and the Marquette Iron Range.

A crew for an ore extra is called when there are enough loads at Eagle Mills for a train, and it is known that there will be enough loaded cars for the second run of the crew. The Chief Dispatcher is responsible for this function.

Motive power assigned to ore extras varies with the following combinations: two 1,500 or 1600 Horse Power Alco Roadswitchers, a 1500 or 1600 HP Alco with a General Electric U 25 C or U 25 C's. It is very rare that a 3 unit combination is used between Eagle Mills and Marquette. Train lengths will usually be 110 cars with such combinations, but two U 25 C's can handle up to 140 cars. Every so often, when there is a rush of vessels at the dock and power is short, one will see a single U 25 C with about 80 cars.

Each of the two trips between Marquette and Eagle Mills takes about four hours. Often, on the first trip of the crew, they will run all the way to Negaunee and set out their entire train at Harris Yard. The crew will then return light to Eagle Mills, place their caboose on the rear of their ore train, couple the locomotive on the train, build up the air to 75 pounds of pressure, test the brakes and return to Marquette.

DURING THE DAYS OF STEAM, the Lake Superior & Ishpeming Railroad used 2-10-2's on their road trains. Here is Ore Extra 37 East rolling toward Marquette with a loaded train.—*Courtesy Lake Superior & Ishpeming*

THE LAKE SUPERIOR & ISHPEMING ore train arriving at the ore yard in Marquette.—*Courtesy James Smeberg*

Enroute, the LS&I has a spectacular steel deck viaduct which is 110 feet above the churning Dead River. There is a 20 MPH speed limit over the bridge.

There is a home signal at the entrance to the Marquette ore dock yard. This signal governs the movement of trains into the arrival yard. The arrival yard is made up of three tracks, all of which diverge off the main line. The LS&I has remote control switches for these arrival tracks, which are under the jurisdiction of the dispatcher at the ore yard. Thus arriving ore trains do not have to stop for the head brakeman to jump off and run ahead to throw switches for the train. The train rolls right into the track set up by the dispatcher and stops after the conductor on the caboose has radioed the engineer that the rear of the train has cleared the main line. All LS&I motive power and cabooses are equipped with radios and the crew can talk with each other and with the dispatcher at any time. Upon arrival, the engine is cut off from the train. The engine crew then runs around the ore train and picks up the conductor and rear-end brakeman. The crew then heads for the roundhouse where they eat lunch if it's their first trip, and tie up if it is their second trip. The road haul completes two thirds of the LS&I's responsibility of the ore from mine to dock.

Ore Dock and Yard Operations

The LS&I maintains a 17 track classification yard, with a capacity of 1,092 ore cars; a 3 track arrival yard with individual track capacity of 125 cars each; a 3 track departure yard with track capacities of 115 cars, 118 cars and 125 cars; and a 1200 foot ore dock with a ca-

pacity of 50,000 tons at Marquette for their final movement of the ore from mine to ship. The LS&I also has two hot houses for thawing frozen ore, each facility capable of thawing 56 cars at a time. In addition, the LS&I's car and locomotive shops are located at this yard.

There are three basic types of switching assignments at this yard. The first assignment is the ore dock pusher. This crew is responsible for ore classification and for placing ore cars in 20 to 30 car blocks on the top of the ore dock. There are one to three of these assignments on each shift. The second type is a tramp assignment which classifies ore, shoves on the ore dock, switches industries and delivers ore to and from the Soo Line. These two assignments are also responsible for the assembly of empty ore trains for Eagle Mills. The third assignment is the coal dock assignment, and operates only when there is a boat unloading coal at the Marquette Dock Company.

Since the Fall of 1967, the LS&I has had in operation a high speed scale at Eagle Mills with an Automatic Car Identification System. The cars are weighed during departure from Eagle Mills and the ACI System works in exactly the same way as described in the chapter on the DM&IR. Thus there is no weighing of ore in the ore dock yard as there is in other ore dock yard operations.

Classification of ore is now at a minimum because of the increased amount of pellets. The pellets are a uniform product and the need for mixing on the ore dock is not as great now as it was several years ago.

To understand the complexities ore mixing presented for the LS&I—and still does present to the Great Northern, Duluth, Missabe & Iron Range, Soo Line, Northern Pacific and the Candian National and will continue to do so until their pellet shipments exceed the amount of raw ore shipped—Let's go back to 1960 and the LS&I ore dock operations at that time.

In 1960, the LS&I handled the following types of ore: Athens, Maas, Mather A and B, Ohio, Champion, Greenwood, Morris, Tilden, Tracy, Cliff Crushed, Cliff Lump, Humboldt Concentrate and Pellets, and Improved Ore No. 1, 3, and 4. In addition, the LS&I delivered to the ex-Duluth, South Shore & Atlantic Railway for further handling Improved Ore. No. 5 and 6.

The improved ores mentioned above are:

Group 1—Fine ore resulting from drying and screening raw Mather A, Mather B, Maas or Athens.

Group 3—Raw Mather A and B, Maas or Athens dried.

Group 4—Coarse ore resulting from drying and screening raw Mather A, B, Maas or Athens.

Group 5—Fine ore resulting from drying and screening Tracy ore.

Group 6—Coarse ore resulting from drying and screening Tracy ore.

Ordinarily Group 1, Group 4, Cliff lump and Tilden ores were not mixed, but were shipped as either a full cargo or as a compartment in a boat.

The other ores were mixed or blended in accordance with steel company specifications.

Let's take a look at a single boat load during 1960 and see how it was handled. On July 5th, the Great Lakes ore carrier, the International, arrived at the LS&I dock at 1:00 a.m. The cargo was made up of the following ores:

Cars	Kind	Lot Nos.
30	Crushed	Lots 9528, 9530, 9531, 10 each.
40	Mather A	Lots 664, 668, 669, 671, 10 each.
27	Mather B	Lots 2662, 2665, 10 each. Lot 2666, 7 cars.
55	No. 3	Lots 9449, 9450, 9451, 9452, 9453, 10 each.
40	Maas	Lots 5582, 5583, 5586, 10 each. Lots 5584, 5587, 5 cars.
10	Morris	Lots 763 and 764, 5 cars each.
9	Ohio	Lot 50.

Total number of cars—211.

When the above information reached the ore dock office, the ore dock agent made plans for laying out the cargo for this particular ship. In this case, since each ore dock pocket holds four cars, it was necessary to use fifty pockets and hold 11 cars to finish the boat. It is necessary to hold a certain number of cars in order to properly distribute the boat load. One

THE LAKE SUPERIOR & ISHPEMING uses many different types of locomotives for their Marquette ore yard and dock switching service. This view shows a General Electric 2250 HP U23C preparing to shove a train onto the ore dock.—*Courtesy James Smeberg*

thing that must be taken into consideration is the placing of the cargo in certain pockets of the dock so that loading of other boats will not be interfered with.

After it has been decided which pockets will be used, the ore cars are placed on the ore dock and dumping begins. As much as possible, the first cars of ore dumped in a pocket was—and still is—an ore which runs freely and will start the ore going down the chute. This ore is always dumped from the inside track into the pocket to spread it as much as possible.

In the example cited above, the first cars in the fifty pockets would be the 30 crushed, the 9 Ohio and 11 group No. 3. The second cars in the pocket would be 44 group No. 3 and 6 Mather A. The third cars in the pocket would be 16 Mather B and 34 Maas. The fourth cars in the pocket would be 34 Mather A, 6 Maas and 10 Morris. Eleven cars of Mather B were held for finishing. In this manner, the cargo of ore is well mixed.

Upon the arrival of the vessel, the chutes on the ore dock are lowered into the hold of the vessel and the ore flows into the boat. It may take anywhere from 2 to 5 hours to load a vessel at the LS&I dock.

At the present time, there are fewer mines operating but there is a greater tonnage of pellets coming from the mines and plants that are operating. There is still a considerable amount of mixing on the LS&I dock, but this amount is declining as the tonnage of pellets increases year after year.

After the ore cars are unloaded on the dock, the pusher engine pulls them down to the yard, switches out the bad orders or damaged cars, and places the rest of the cars in one of the departure tracks. When one of these tracks is full, the Chief Dispatcher calls a crew for an ore extra to Eagle Mills or Harris Yard at Negaunee, provided a train load is ready at Eagle Mills.

There are two other operations at the Mar-

A VIEW of the LS&I ore dock in Marquette.

THIS STRING of ore cars has just arrived off the ore dock. The bad orders will now be switched out and the other cars placed in the departure yard.—*Courtesy James Smeberg*

quette Ore Yard that play a part in the movement of iron ore through the port. One is the transfer of ore and/or pellets to the Soo Line. The other is the late fall or early spring thawing of frozen ore in both the ore cars and the LS&I and Soo Line ore docks.

With the increasing tonnage resulting at the LS&I ore dock, ore or pellets that cannot be handled efficiently is transferred to the Soo Line freight yard by the tramp assignment. Trains of up to 80 cars of ore and pellets per day are sent to the Soo account of overflow or steel company specifications of mixing pellets with Tracy ore on the Soo Dock. The transfer of ore to the Soo Line is usually made in the morning, and the Soo has the empties returned to the LS&I in the late afternoon.

As previously mentioned, the LS&I maintains two heating houses for thawing frozen cars of ore or pellets. Each house is capable of thawing 56 cars at a time. When the ore or pellets have frozen inside the ore dock, the LS&I uses two cars equipped with a type CFK 4225 Vapor Clarkson Steam Generator. One car is a rebuilt tender from a steam locomotive, and the other is a flat car with a large water tank mounted on the car with a steam generator on one end. Both cars must be used with a 1000 HP Alco Road Switcher for their electrical power. When the cars are needed for slushing service on either dock, they can be steamed up in 15 minutes compared to 2 or more hours for steaming up a steam locomotive. The LS&I supplies the equipment for the ore car thawing and ore dock slushing for themselves and the Soo Line. However, the Soo does their own thawing and slushing.

The ore dock operations are the last phase in the transportation of iron ore from Michigan Mines to the steel mills for the LS&I. The LS&I ore dock is the oldest concrete ore dock on the Great Lakes. It was built in 1912. As concrete keeps getting harder for the first 100 years of its life, one can expect that the dock has many years of life ahead of it—especially since the mining expansion on the Marquette Iron Range keep rolling along.

Other Road Operations

During the winter season, the LS&I operates a number of all rail ore trains to connections with the Soo Line and the Chicago & North Western Railway. The destination of these ore trains is generally either the Detroit or Chicago Areas.

The longest run on the LS&I is the all-rail movement of ore or pellets from Eagle Mills to either Eben Junction (Soo connection) or Lit-

AN 1800 HP ROADSWITCHER—These locomotives are generally assigned to mine transfer service and to the ore dock. One of these locomotives has been rebuilt to a 2000 HP unit with a cut down nose.—*Courtesy Alco Products*

tle Lake (C&NW connection). Such operations generally begin shortly after the closing of the shipping season.

When such trains are operated, the procedure goes something like this. After the winter day trick switching operations have been completed on the Marquette Range between Eagle Mills and Republic, some of the motive power is used to make up a 3 unit locomotive for the ore extra. The crew is normally called for around 5 p.m. The crew reports to the Eagle Mills Engine House and they pick up their orders at that point. The crew then takes the locomotive to the outbound yard and couples on to their train. When the air brakes have been tested and the train inspection made, the train departs for one of the two above named connections.

Upon arrival at Marquette, the ore crew must determine whether or not the East End local has arrived at the yard. If it has not yet arrived at Marquette, the crew receives orders as to where they should meet the local.

Since it is winter, and this is heavy snow country, the motive power has a pilot mounted snow plow. This plow is used almost constantly during the eastbound run, being lifted only to cross streets and highways. The snow fall in this area averages nearly 200 inches per winter. The engines must really work to plow the snow and pull the ore train. The snow often flies over the cab of the lead unit, blocking out all view for a moment or two.

When the ore train arrives at the connection, they set out their train in the yard tracks. If there are empty ore cars in the yard being returned from Chicago or elsewhere, the crew gathers up the ore cars and returns to Mar-

quette. At Marquette, the ore cars are set out where they are inspeccted the next day and the bad orders are switched to the shops. The crew then either continues on to Eagle Mills light or picks up another train of empties for Eagle Mills. The entire run takes from 8 to 12 hours to complete. Upon arrival at Eagle Mills, the motive power is readied for the day trick switching assignments on the Range. In this way, the LS&I obtains maximum utilization for its diesel power.

The Future

The future of the LS&I as an ore carrying road has never been brighter. Pellet production is increasing on the Marquette Range, and the major portion of this is shipped over the LS&I to Marquette. The LS&I presently has plans for building a storage area adjacent to the ore dock at Marquette. A conveyor system, similar to the Great Northern arrangement at Superior, (which will be described in the chapter on the Great Northern) for transporting the pellets to the dock during the shipping season and a storage area is in the planning stage. In this manner, the LS&I management will be able to operate their railroad full time on a year around basis instead of the present 8 month rush. This will provide stable employment and will bolster the economy of Marquette during the winter.

And so goes the LS&I, its present operations are highly efficient and its plans for the future operations are many under the able leadership of a fine management. The officers, staff and employees of the LS&I have shown an outstanding display of teamwork that has produced a profitable railroad, and has contributed much to the American Economy.

A BUILDER'S PHOTO of one of the two U25C's that the LS&I uses on the ore trains. These locomotives are seldom used on the ore dock assignments. On the road trains, they are usually MU'd with an Alco 1600 HP road switcher.—*Courtesy General Electric*

THE LS&I ordered 200 of these cars in 1957. Many of these were rebuilt with extensions for pellet service. Also, a fleet of these cars without extensions are used in concentrate ore service from the Republic mine to the Pioneer.—*Courtesy Bethlehem Steel Company*

100 OF THESE CARS were purchased by the LS&I in 1964. They are the largest capacity cars ever built for ore service in the Lake Superior region. These cars were also the first cars that were not built in the traditional way of ore car construction. Note that these cars look more like shortened coal hoppers instead of ore cars.—*Courtesy Bethlehem Steel Company*

THE LAKE SUPERIOR & ISHPEMING has not purchased any new cabooses during the last few years. However, they have rebuilt many of their older ones. Here is a view of a typical rebuilt caboose. —*Courtesy James Smeberg*

THESE WERE THE LAST ore cars ordered by any railroad in the Lake Superior region. These cars are used by the LS&I in both pellet and raw ore service.—*Courtesy Bethlehem Steel Company*

Chapter Four

The Great Northern Railway

ET US IMAGINE for a moment that you are a Great Northern locomotive engineer at the Allouez Ore Dock Yard. You have been called to work a day shift assignment on the ore docks. At the yard office, you meet the rest of the crew and exchange a few words and then go out to the locomotive. You have a big 1,750 HP, SD-9 on two six-wheeled trucks. The conductor has the orders from the yard master as to which block of cars you will shove on the ore dock first. You pull the throttle out a couple of notches as the conductor signals you to move down to the classification yard. The switchmen line switches and you arrive on a track with 40 cars of ore waiting to be shoved on the No. 4 ore dock. You couple up, the air is cut in and you open the throttle to the 4th notch to pump up the air in the train. After the air is pumped up, you set the brakes for a test. After the OK is given, you wait for a yellow signal to proceed toward the dock. You receive it, you open the throttle to the eighth notch, the sand is turned on and you begin pushing 4,000 gross tons up hill. Your fireman yells clear on the Omaha (The C&NW is still known as the Omaha in former Omaha Territory), as the home signal for the C&NW crossing comes into view. The sand is still on, the ore ore cars are going up hill, a red over yellow signal comes into view. With the sand still on, the ore cars begin to swing to the right through the interlocking limits, on to the No. 4 ore dock approach. You are almost to the top now and the sand can be turned off, and the throttle dropped to the 6th notch. You begin rolling on the dock, you push the throttle to the second notch. The conductor gives you the five car lengths sign, you shut the throttle, apply air, four car lengths, 3, 2, 1, stop. The air is escaping loudly—the train stops over the right dock pockets.

The Great Northern Railway moves iron ore from the Mesabi Range to the Superior, Wisconsin ore docks for about a dozen mining companies. The companies load ore at approximately 50 points on the Great Northern.

The mining companies ship about 50 different grades of ore over the GN. Because of the varied chemical and other properties of the Mesabi and Cuyuna Range ores, the mixing and blending of these ores for a particular steel company's needs are of great importance. After the ore is loaded into the ore cars, samples are taken from groups of three to seven cars. The samples are analyzed so the mining companies can determine how many ore cars from various mines should be blended to make up a particular grade. The mining companies then tell the GN which cars go into which boats. This is accomplished by assigning a block number to groups of carloads. This block number designates a boat and in some cases it also has a suffix letter, A, B, C or D; which designates the dumping order into the ore dock pocket. Each road train normally contains cars for about 15 or 16 blocks, and has to be cut 20 to 23 times during classification at the Allouez hump yard (Superior, Wisconsin ore dock yard). Some cars will not fit any particular block being accumulated, so they are set aside and classified later when a block is assigned. After the cars of ore are classified and sorted, they are shoved to the docks in cuts of 40 cars.

Teletype is used to transmit train consists as soon as an ore train departs the Range, and to transmit back grade messages so block numbers can be assigned the cars.

In the ore operations, radio is used very extensively. All mine run, road haul and yard engines are radio equipped. All road haul and mine run cabooses have radio. In addition, several wayside stations in ore territory, such as

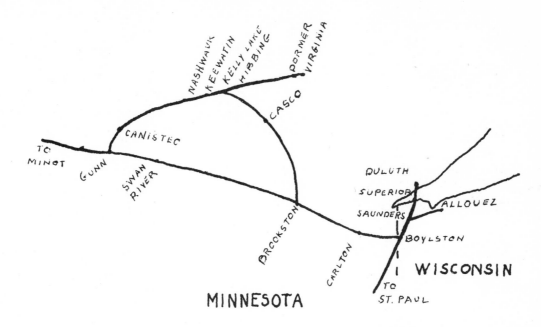

Not To Scale

Saunders, Brookston, Grand Rapids, and Kelly Lake Yard, have radio.

The Great Northern ore movement can be divided into three coordinated segments, the mine run transfer service, road haul and ore dock classification and boat loading.

Mine Transfer Service

Under the supervision of the Chief Dispatcher and a Trainmaster, this operation includes the movement of empty cars from the points where set out by road trains to the mines or taconite plants, and the return of loaded ore cars to the build up points for movement by road train back to Superior. Road trains are made up at Canisteo, Calumet and Nashwauk. Most of the mines served by the Great Northern are between Gunn and Buhl. The Chief Dispatcher's main function is to distribute empties to the mines according to the mining company's need. The over all daily allotment of cars to the mines is given to the Chief Dispatcher by the Ore Dock Superintendent.

Mine run transfers are handled by single unit SD-7's or 9's (EMD 1500 HP or 1750 HP road switcher types respectively). In the mining territory, i.e., between Kelly Lake and Dormer Jct., transfers and road trains must comply with Consolidated Rule No. 93. This means that they must move being prepared to stop at any time for yard engines, etc. The primary purpose of the mine run transfers is the distribution of empties and the assembly of road trains. The mine run assignments work the entire line between Virginia and Canisteo.

Road Trains

Ore extras generally consist of 205 cars loaded. Empties have run as much as 250 in one train. The crews begin their trip at the Superior Roundhouse and go over to the Allouez ore yard by way of Saunders. The crews work in a turnaround, making the round trip of over 200 miles in about 10 to 12 hours. The Chief Dispatcher at Superior (Superior is the headquarters for the Mesabi Division) is responsible for the road movement and coordinates the need for empties or loads with the Mesabi Range on one hand and the docks on the other. Normal locomotive consists are usually three units for ore trains. The consist may have 3 F-7 units, but with the F-T's, F-3's and F-7's being traded in for high horsepower geeps, it is not uncommon to see a lash up of a GP-30 or 35 and 2 F-7's. Such a combination makes quite a unique sound as they wind up to 50 MPH, speed limit for empty ore cars. The speed

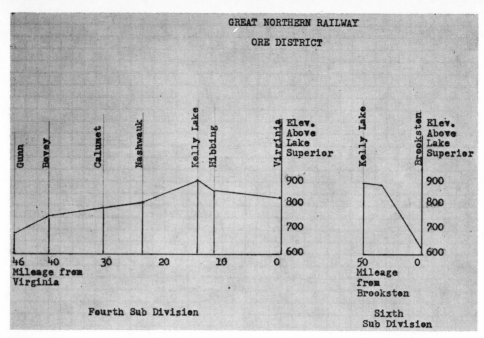

Fourth Sub Division

Sixth Sub Division

limit for loaded ore cars is 30 MPH on main lines and 20 MPH on branch lines.

The line from Saunders to Brookston is double track. From Brookston to both Kelly Lake and Gunn is CTC controlled from the Superior office. The entire CTC district covers 99.5 miles. The Great Northern installed CTC in the ore district in 1959. Prior to 1960, ore traffic moved over three heavy north-south lines. CTC permitted the abandonment of the middle line, which consisted of 23.2 route miles plus two sidings and a pole line. Also it permitted removal of 28.4 miles of second track from the Duluth-Superior-Minot main line, retaining about 8 miles of second track for long passing sidings. Thus CTC helped reduce maintenance costs and gave greater flexibility in ore operations. Empties move north on the Casco line rather than over the abandoned Swan River route. Before CTC was installed, empty cars moved up the Swan River line and loads rolled down either of the outer lines. Routing decisions were determined by the area in which the empties were needed and the loads were originating. However, a prevailing direction of traffic was maintained over the three lines. Now with CTC, the dispatcher has a complete picture of the operations of the lines. He can plan meets with much flexibility and delay is minimized. CTC also assists the dispatcher in giving the local freight train in the ore territory as much track occupancy as it needs with a high degree of safety. The CTC does not cover the mining region itself, but only the long haul from the Mesabi Range to the double track on the main line at Brookston.

The Mesabi Division is one of the busiest divisions on the Great Northern. Between Boylston and Saunders, there are four regular passenger trains, eight regular freights and 10 to 16 ore trains daily including the unit tarconite train. In addition, there are numerous grain and coal trains when traffic warrants the extras. The Mesabi Division handles some of the heaviest trains of the entire world, and does so day in and day out with completely safety. The Great Northern takes it as a matter of course, whereas people from other parts of the country look twice when they hear about or see a 20,000 ton train.

Yard Classification and Dock Operations

Allouez Yard might be called the hub of the entire Great Northern operation of ore hauling. Over 15 million tons of ore per year flow through the docks and if the flow stops at Allouez, everything stops. The yard has a capacity of 8,000 ore cars and has over 40 miles of track. It has a 19 track receiving yard, a 9 track departure yard, an 89 track classification yard with track capacities of 25 to 45 cars, and two small yards for handling interchange ore with the Northern Pacific-Soo Line operation. The Great Northern interchanges ore with the DM&IR at Saunders.

The General Yardmaster has the responsibility of the humping and classification of the road trains. The cars are weighed automatically while being humped. As each car nears the crest of the hump and on to the scale, a console operator punches on a keyboard the car number. A Univac computer pulls the tare weight of the car from its memory and a tape is punched in the ore dock office showing the net weight of the ore in the car. This tape is then used to produce punch cards to be used for records such as, block lists, mine waybills and ore vessel reports.

The classification of ore cars is coordinated with dock requirements by the Ore Dock Superintendent, who supervises the dumping of ore into the dock and loading of boats. Roadswitcher type locomotives, SD-7's and 9's are used to shove cuts of 40 cars or so and spot over specific pockets on the dock upon the direction of the Ore Dock Office.

After the crew has spotted their loads, they may either return to the yard light or gather up empties. When they gather up empties, they frequently make up trains of over 100 cars for movement to the departure yard. At the departure yard, the crew switches out the bad order cars and the foreign cars. The latter are then returned to the interchanges. The Great Northern cars are then made up into 205 car trains and readied for return to the Mesabi Range.

There are three types of switching assignments at the Allouez Yard. One is the transfer engine. This crew works between Allouez Yard and Saunders handling the DM&IR interchange ore. It also goes to Saunders to switch trains, such as No. 414 from Minot, if that particular train is carrying ore. This writer has seen No. 414 arrive at Saunders with as many as 40 cars of ore on the head-end.

Another assignment is the hump engine. This crew is responsible for taking each train and shoving over the hump for weighing and classification. It is interesting to note that at the time of this writing hump riders are still used at Allouez. The Great Northern takes special care in the training of these hump riders. The safety record of these men has been tremendous.

The last assignment is the ore dock shove engine. The ore dock assignment has a regular system to follow. The crew makes a total of four shoves on to the dock and two pulls. This is the reason why shoves will be around 40, but the pulls from the dock will be 80 to 125 empties.

In the days of steam, the GN used 0-8-0's steam switchers on the ore docks. These engines were able to push 37 cars on to the docks.

Next to the classification yard is a little used facility, but extremely important to the operation. That facility is the steam plant and yard. Prior to 1943, steam locomotives were used around the classification yard to thaw frozen ore cars in the early winter and early spring. However, the brutal war year of 1943 needed every steam locomotive for pulling troops and military supplies, etc. Therefore, in 1943 a stationary plant was built and remodeled in 1953. The facility consists of two boilers

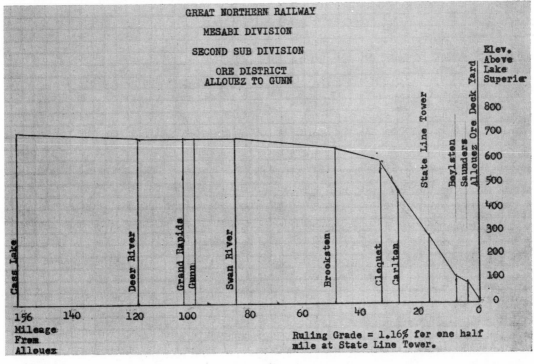

each capable of producing 48,000 pounds of steam per hour. Steam lines are run from these boilers to the steaming holes on the sides of the ore cars. After the loads are thawed, there is a big rush to get the cars to the dock for dumping. After the car has been dumped and the pocket filled, if the ore freezes in the dock, steam must again be used to get the frozen ore out of the dock pocket and into an ore boat. This is called slushing and now boiler cars and steam locomotive tenders for water are used for this service.

The Ore Docks

The Great Northern has three operating ore docks. The three docks have a total capacity of 344,000 tons and a total of 1,026 ore pockets. There is 200 feet between docks and each dock is long enough to load two boats on a side simultaneously. Cargoes vary from 10,000 to 25,000 tons—and will soon be even larger as the 900 to 1000 foot long ore carriers are launched. The average time that a boat spends at a GN dock is around 5½ hours.

Ore dock forces work seven days a week on all shifts because of the around-the-clock demands of ship arrivals and departures.

The Taconite Story

A little round ball of processed taconite with a high percentage of iron in the content is now making itself known to more and more railroaders. Its production has meant new life to the Great Northern ore operations. Two plants on the GN are now producing pellets from taconite ore. The GN prepared for this operation with the construction of a new bulk storage facility next to the ore classification yard at Allouez. The facility permits taconite unit trains to operate on a year around basis instead of seasonally. A storage area for about 2.2 million tons of pellets has been built and can be expected to accommodate 5 million tons. A 2.1 mile system of conveyor belts has been built to transport the pellets from the storage area to the No. 1 ore dock.

The ore cars used in taconite service have been rebuilt with 18 inch extensions so that they can carry a 75 ton pay load. Pellets take up more space than ore of the same weight.

Let's take a look at how the Great Northern uses these tools to handle a train load of taconite pellets.

There are two plants on the GN. One is located at Nashwauk and the other at Keewatin. The two plants ship pellets on alternate days—seven days a week.

When the empty taconite ore cars have been inspected and so forth, a crew is called for a run to one of the above mentioned plants. The motive power is a four unit F-7. The crew reports to the Superior round house and takes the locomotive to the Allouez Yard. They couple on to the train, which incidentally has a new steel bay window caboose, and depart for the Range. The run to one of the two plants takes about 3 to 4 hours of running time. Upon arrival at the plant, the engine proceeds through the loading facility with the cars at the amazing speed of ½ mile per hour. The loading is nonstop and it stakes about 2 hours and 45 minutes to load 200 cars. The reason bay window cabooses are used on the taconite assignments is that a cupola caboose would not clear the loading chutes. The train, after loading, continues on toward Gunn and back to Superior.

Upon arrival at Allouez, the train remains fully coupled except for the road locomotive, which is not used for unloading. The first two cars of the train are spotted right at the unloading station by the road engine. A machine, without a switch engine, then advances the train through the unloading station at the rate of 40 cars per hour or in terms of tonnage, 3,000 tons per hour. The cars are positioned for dumping two at a time.

During the shipping season, the pellets will move directly from the unloading point via conveyor belt to the ore dock. This conveyor

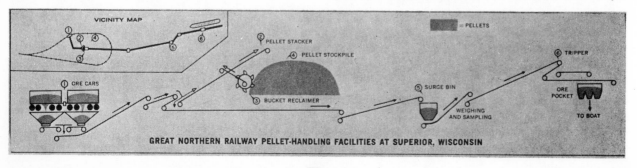

GREAT NORTHERN RAILWAY PELLET-HANDLING FACILITIES AT SUPERIOR, WISCONSIN

belt extends to the end of the No. 1 ore dock. Enroute the pellets are automatically weighed and sampled. On the dock a belt feeder with a tripper on a boom deposits the taconite pellets into any of the 374 pockets. Each pocket has a capacity of 300 tons of pellets compared to 350 tons of raw ore. The pellets are loaded into ore vessels in the usual manner.

During the winter, the pellets are stockpiled on the ground in the storage area. A huge 85 foot stacker, which is mounted on a 3,000 foot section of rail and equipped with a 160 foot boom conveyor, deposits each individual plant's production in piles up to 50 feet high. When shipping resumes in the spring, pellets stockpiled during the winter are gradually removed

by a bucket wheel reclaimer and deposited directly on the main belt moving to the ore dock. And when the pellets are loaded into a waiting vessel, the Great Northern's responsibility for that shipment is complete.

The future of the Great Northern ore operations has never been brighter. In fact it outshines the yellow stripes on the extensions and ends of the rebuilt ore cars. In perhaps 5 to 10 years, the seasonal ore train will be all but gone from the scene. There will, of course, be more trains during the shipping season, but most of the ore trains will roll all winter long to feed the storage area at the Allouez Ore Yard. The future of the Great Northern ore operations is very bright indeed.

A GN ORE TRAIN is departing Kelly Lake yard, during the days of steam, for the railway's ore dock at Allouez.—*Courtesy Great Northern*

THE GREAT NORTHERN used Mallets on their ore runs during the days of steam. Here a 2-8-8-0 heads toward Allouez with 160 cars in tow.—*Courtesy Wayne C. Olsen*

THE GREAT NORTHERN had a fleet of 25 type N-2's, wheel arrangement 2-8-8-0, all of which were used in Mesabi Division ore service. These locomotives weighed 286 tons.—*Courtsy Wayne C. Olsen*

TODAY, 3 UNIT F-7's handle most of the ore traffic between Allouez and the Mesabi Range. This train is eastbound on the Second Subdivision about 2½ miles east of Brookston, Minnesota.—*Courtesy Great Northern*

GREAT NORTHERN Extra 317 A West passes Saunders Tower enroute to the Mesabi Range with 202 empties.

WEIGHING IRON ORE "on the fly" at Great Northern Railway's Allouez yards, en route to the docks, at Superior, Wisconsin.—*Courtesy Great Northern Railway*

AT GREAT NORTHERN RAILWAY'S iron ore classification yards near its Allouez docks at Superior, Wisconsin, train loads of ore arrive from Minnesota mines. In the yards cars containing various types of ore are arranged in short trains before being taken to the docks for transfer to Great Lakes boats. This gives steamers the cargo composition desired by the ore receivers when the vessels reach their eastern destinations.—*Courtesy Great Northern Railway*

THE GREAT NORTHERN'S Allouez ore yard has a double track hump. Here seven cars are rolling off the hump through a crossover and into the classification yard.

THE GREAT NORTHERN inter-
changes ore with the Duluth, Missabe & Iron Range Railway at
Saunders, Wisconsin. A transfer
crew from Allouez is arriving at
Saunders with 162 DM&IR empties. Because of the trackage arrangement, DM&IR crews must
back into and out of this yard
when their trains arrive with ore.

SD-7 NO. 563 is struggling very hard with 50 loads for the No. 4 ore dock. Fifty loads can be
shoved onto the No. 4 dock because it is slightly lower than either the No. 1 or No. 2.

IN THE DAYS OF STEAM, the GN used 0-8-0's for switching the ore docks. Here is the 837 shoving 37 cars onto the No. 1 ore dock.—*Courtesy Wayne C. Olsen*

OFTEN IRON ORE is quite reluctant to flow easily from the ore car into the dock pocket. When this happens, the Great Northern has a traveling car shaker. It is shown here working on a car of stubborn ore.—*Courtesy Great Northern*

THIS VIEW on top of the No. 2 ore dock at Allouez shows the dock pockets. When a train arrives on the dock, as shown here, the cars are spotted directly over designated pockets. The hopper doors are then opened and the ore flows into the pockets, where it will stay until the arrival of a ship.
—*Courtesy Great Northern*

CHUTING IRON ORE into the hold of a Great Lakes carrier at Great Northern Railway's Allouez docks at Superior, Wisconsin. —*Courtesy Great Northern Railway*

IRON ORE SLIDES into a Great Lakes carrier for the eastward voyage at Great Northern Railway's Allouez docks at Superior, Wisconsin.—*Great Northern Railway.*

A VIEW of the No. 4 ore dock from the ore superintendent's office. Note the partially dismantled No. 3 to the left.

HERE IS AN OLDER VIEW of the Great Northern ore docks before the flood lights and overhead car shakers were installed. —*Courtesy Great Northern Railway*

THE GREAT NORTHERN ore docks operate on a 24 hour, daily schedule. The flood lights shown here on the No. 1 ore dock, completely light up the entire dock for safe, around the clock operation. —*Courtesy Great Northern Railway*

THE GREAT NORTHERN RAILWAY'S Allouez docks at Superior, Wisconsin are, together, the largest installation of ore loading docks in the world. They have facilities for berthing 18 ore carriers at one time and loading 12 simultaneously. This view shows the No. 2 ore dock. The No. 3 can be seen in the right hand of the photo. This ore dock has now been dismantled, which leaves only 3 docks, the Nos. 1, 2 and 4. The No. 3 was a timber dock and was the last one on Lake Superior.—*Courtesy Great Northern Railway*

THE OPERATIONS of the GN's docks at Superior are directed from this office and general service building. The structure rests on steel towers and is 78 feet above the water. A complete view of the 3 ore docks is provided from the second floor, which is on a level with the upper dock platforms and tracks on which ore trains arrive. This picture, taken from the land side, shows the rear of the building.—*Courtesy Great Northern*

THE GREAT NORTHERN RAILWAY'S No. 1 ore dock is shown here loading a Reiss Steamship Company ship with a cargo of ore.—*Courtesy Great Northern Ry.*

EVERY SHIPPING SEASON, the ore docks take a terrific beating from the flow of iron ore through the pockets and chutes. Consequently, the pocket doors and chutes must be prepared during the winter season. This photo shows the Great Northern No. 1 ore dock during winter repair. One can also see the conveyor system leading to the ore dock and the machine on top of the dock that deposits the pellets into the pockets.

THAWING ORE in the Great Northern yards at Allouez in 1936. This view is identical today, except that instead of steam locomotives, the GN has several stationary boilers in the left side of this photo.—*Courtesy Great Northern*

THE GREAT NORTHERN operates three basic types of ore cars. The first 75 ton cars that were purchased were these slanted end types.

LATER ON, an improvement was made in the design of the 75 ton cars being purchased by the GN. The result was this type of an ore car with an increase in the amount of cubic feet.

PRIOR TO 1943, the Great Northern used steam locomotives for thawing frozen ore. This photo clearly shows the use of piping for this very cold work.—*Courtesy Great Northern*

A BUILDER'S PHOTO of the last type of ore car ordered by the Great Northern. Over 200 of this type have been rebuilt for the taconite service.—*Courtesy ACF Industries*

A GREAT NORTHERN ore train moves under the elevated conveyor belt system and the cars are automatically filled with taconite pellets. When loaded, the train will leave Minnesota's Iron Range for the Allouez docks in Superior, Wisconsin.—*Great Northern Railway*

LOADED IN TRANSIT, specially built ore cars move under the loading facility at the Butler taconite plant operated by the Hanna Mining Company near Nashwauk, Minnesota. The plant has a projected annual capacity of 2 million tons of pellets, primarily for Inland Steel Corporation and Wheeling Steel Corporation. GN has constructed seven miles of new spur tracks to serve this facility and another at Keewatin. The pellets are moved to GN's 6 million dollar pellet handling installation at Superior, Wisconsin, where the cars are automatically unloaded onto an intricate conveyor belt system. The pellets are either stockpiled or are fed directly into the hold of the Great Lakes ore boats.

IT TAKES approximately 2 hours and 45 minutes for loading 200 cars. There are only two bay window cabooses in service on the Great Northern. A cupola will not clear the plant loading spouts.

HERE IS A VIEW of the interior of the dumping house at Allouez. The men at the left operate both the dumping mechanism and the train positioner.—*Courtesy Duluth News Tribune*

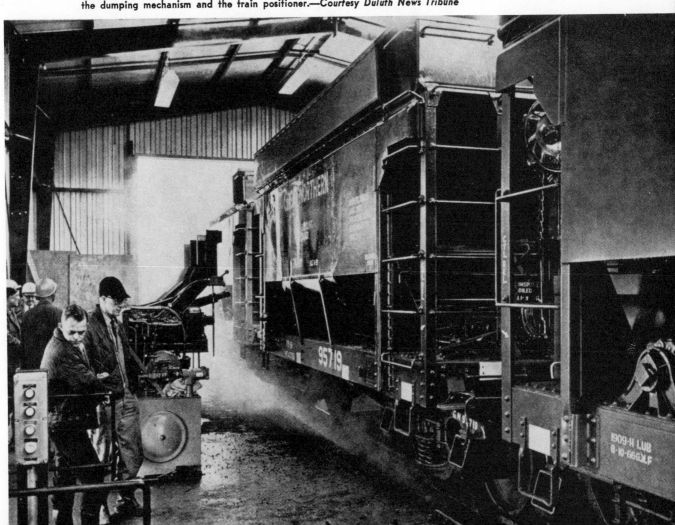

A GREAT NORTHERN RAILWAY unit trainload of taconite pellets—200 cars long and carrying 15,000 tons of pellets—moves along a wide curve from the Hanna Company's Butler taconite plant at Nashwauk, Minnesota. Bound for GN's 6-million-dollar taconite pellet handling facility at Superior, Wisconsin, it will make the 230-mile round-trip from 13 to 14 hours, including loading time. The cargo will be dumped automatically, two at a time, into an underground hopper and onto an intricate conveyor belt system for loading into hold of Great Lakes ore boats.—*Courtesy Great Northern*

THIS IS THE STACKER that deposits the pellets into stockpiles during the winter months at Allouez. The Chicago & North Western will have a similar machine at Escanaba when their installation is completed.—*Courtesy Duluth News Tribune*

A MAMMOTH STOCKPILING machine dominates the scene at Great Northern Railway's 6-million-dollar taconite pellet-handling facility at Superior, Wisconsin. One of the conveyor belts is shown moving taconite pellets where they are stockpiled by the 85-foot stacker and 160-foot boom. GN's unit trains from the Butler taconite plant, operated by the Hanna Company near Nashwauk, Minnesota, arrive with 15,000 tons making the 230-mile round-trip in an estimated 13 to 14 hours, including loading time. The facility accommodates 2,200,000 tons of pellets, but expansion allows for $5\frac{1}{2}$ million tons in storage. From here the pellets are recovered automatically and sent by conveyor to the ore dock for loading into Great Lakes boats.—*Courtesy Great Northern*

THE GREAT NORTHERN'S taconite pellet storage area is located over two miles from the ore dock. The storage area is connected to the ore dock by a conveyor belt, which must be elevated for part of the way in order to cross city streets.

THE FLOW OF TACONITE pellets from the Great Northern's storage facility to the ore dock is regulated by this machine. Weighing of the pellets is done immediately to the left of the surge tank, as this machine is called.

THIS IS THE MACHINE that deposits the taconite pellets into the pockets on the ore dock. The tracks to the right serve the pockets on the right hand side of the dock. There are 187 pockets on each side of the No. 1 ore dock.

MARBLE-SIZED PELLETS of taconite fill the 374 pockets of Great Northern Railway's Dock No. 1 at Superior, Wisconsin, each pocket having a capacity of 275 tons. As Great Lakes ore boats dock alongside, workmen trip the lever mechanism lowering chutes above boat holds and the pellets are deposited.

THE HISTORIC MOMENT of loading the first boat load of taconite pellets at the Great Northern's No. I ore dock at Allouez. The steamer *Joseph H. Thompson* loaded in a very heavy fog on April 14, 1967.—*Courtesy Duluth News Tribune*

A WORKMAN trips a lever atop Dock No. 1 at Great Northern Railway's Allouez dock in Superior, Wisconsin, lowering a chute above one of the holds of the Hanna Company's *Joseph H. Thompson* ore boat. Taconite pellets then roll from the ore dock pockets into the craft. Six hours later, she sailed from Superior to Huron, Ohio, with 18,145 tons of taconite pellets.—*Courtesy Great Northern*

THERE ARE ONLY FOUR passenger trains in the Great Northern's ore territory—and then only for a very short distance: Superior to Boylston. Here is No. 24, the Badger at Superior with a consist of an E-7. Baggage car, buffet coach, 2 coaches and an extra dining car for a special party.

Chapter Five

The Menominee Range
The
Chicago and North Western
and the
Milwaukee Road

HE CHICAGO AND NORTH WESTERN Railway's and the Milwaukee Road's iron Ore hauling operations are pooled in the Upper Peninsula of Michigan. Because of this pooling arrangement, the two railroads are covered together in this chapter.

At the present time, all ore hauling by the C&NW and The Milwaukee Road is located in the Central Section of the Upper Peninsula. All of the ore is handled through one port, Escanaba, located on Lake Michigan. The C&NW ore dock at Escanaba is the only ore handling facility on Lake Michigan. This feature makes the ore handling through Escanaba very economically attractive because of a reduced mileage in Lake Transport—which in turn means a faster turn around for ore carriers.

The Milwaukee Road serves mines from Champion to Iron Mountain, a distance of 56 miles. The Milwaukee Road also has a branch from Channing to Kelso Jct. to Iron River, a distance of 37.5 miles.

The C&NW's ore territory extends from Iron River and Crystal Falls to Escanaba via the Ore Line Subdivision, a distance of 98.8 miles including the Crystal Falls Branch line. The rest of the ore territory extends from Antoine to Powers on the Iron River Subdivision, and from Powers to Escanaba on the Escanaba Subdivision, a distance of 52.6 miles. This territory on the Menominee Range is part of the Milwaukee Road-North Western Ore Pooling Agreement. The C&NW also operates a line to Ishpeming from Escanaba, a distance of 65.9 miles. This line serves the Marquette Iron Range. Up until 1966, the C&NW also served the Gogebic Iron Range mines. All the mines on this Range are now closed. The C&NW hauled the Gogebic ore from Ironwood to Escanaba, a distance of 183.2 miles. During the times the mines were operating in the Ironwood area, this was the longest haul of ore from mine to dock in the Lake Superior Region.

Prior to the ore pooling agreement with the C&NW, the Milwaukee Road used to handle all of their ore traffic to Channing and operate over the Escanaba and Lake Superior Railroad to Escanaba. The Milwaukee Road owned complete ore handling facilities at that point, including two ore docks. Each dock contained 240 pockets and was 1,440 feet long pocket to pocket length. Prior to their agreement with the E&LS, the Milwaukee used to haul their ore to Pembine and operated over the Soo Line to Gladstone. The Soo at the turn of the Century owned an ore dock at Gladstone and the Milwaukee Road shipped over the Soo dock.

Approximately six and one half million tons of ore per year are shipped through the Escanaba ore dock. To handle this tonnage, the C&NW owns 2400 70 ton ore cars. Of these, 690 have extensions for handling pellets. The C&NW also has 1050 50 ton ore cars. Six hundred of these cars have extensions. The Milwaukee Road has 794 cars in the 70 ton class with 350 having extensions.

The operations of the C&NW-Milwaukee Road can be broken down into three segments. First, the present pool operatios of the two roads on the Menominee Range. Second, the Marquette Range operations of the C&NW. And third, the Gogebic Range operation of the C&NW to both Escanada and Ashland, Wisconsin. There are also certain other ore operations by the two railroads.

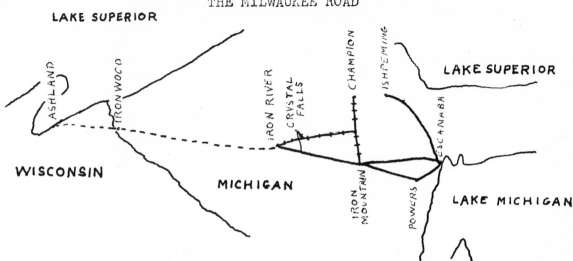

The Menominee Range Ore Pool Agreement

The ore pool agreement was established in the 1930's by the two railroads. It allowed the North Western and the Milwaukee Road to consolidate operations on the Menominee Range. The amount of equipment furnished and man hours worked is directly proportional to the amount of ore handled by each company prior to the application of the Pool Agreement. All of the ore raised on the Menominee Range and shipped out of the C&NW dock at Escanaba is classified Menominee Range ore. The agreement enables the two railroads to handle more efficiently the ore produced on that Range. It is not unusual to see Milwaukee Road diesel units working the C&NW dock or cut in between C&NW units on road ore trains.

The Menominee Range ore is mined in the Stambaugh, Crystal Falls and Iron Mountain areas. Crews from both railroads service the mines, and the ore trains are made up at Stambaugh, Crystal Falls and Iron Mountain. From these three yards, there are approximately four trains per day dispatched to Escanaba. The trains are about 115 cars long and handled by 2 or 3 unit Fairbanks-Morse 1600 HP Baby Trainmaster diesel road switchers. Both roads use the same type of power. These types of diesels are also used for servicing the mines. Before dieselization, C&NW J-4 class 2-8-4's and Milwaukee Road "Mikes" were used over the road, and C&NW Z class 2-8-0 steam power was used for switching and road operations.

The ore trains usually travel over the Ore Line Subdivision enroute to Escanaba. Trains

LEGEND

Not to Scale

—— C&NW Ore Lines

+++ Milw. Rd. Ore Lines

- - - Former C&NW Ore Lines

traveling over this line arrive at the No. 6 Ore yard, where they are classified and stored until movement on to the ore dock. If ore trains are routed over the line via Powers, or if ore is carried in regular freight train No. 36 from Iron Mountain to Powers; and No. 39 from Powers to Escanaba, the ore arrives in the main freight yard near the passenger depot. When the ore arrives in the freight yard, it must be taken to the No. 6 ore yard before it is placed on the ore dock.

The ore is shoved on to the dock with 1600 HP Fairbanks-Morse 6 wheeled Road Switchers. The length of the shove varies from 30 to 60 cars. The ore is dumped into the dock in the same manner as described in the chapter on the DM&IR or LS&I.

The C&NW is now operating the last timber dock on the Great Lakes. The ore dock, known as the No. 6, has 320 pockets of 250 ton capacity and is 1,920 feet long. The total tonnage capacity is 80,000 tons, which makes it the largest of the three ore docks in the State of Michigan.

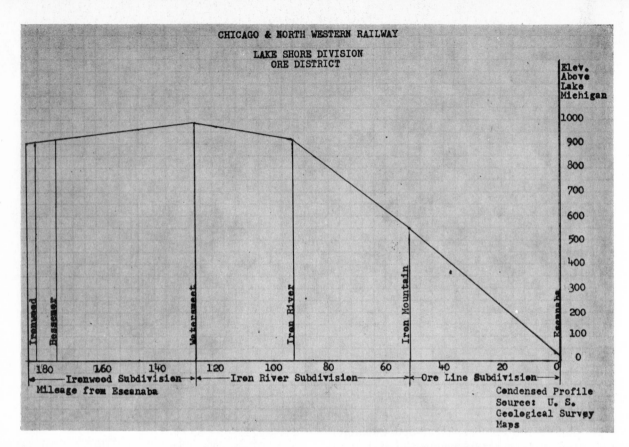

Prior to 1960, the C&NW operated two ore docks at Escanaba. The No. 5 ore dock was 2,220 feet long and contained 370 pockets of 250 ton capacity. This ore dock was dismantled in 1960. Through the improved scheduling of ships, the present No. 6 ore dock is able to handle more ore per year than both docks were able to handle 10 years ago.

When pelletized ore is loaded into the ore cars at Randville or elsewhere, it may be still quite hot from the roasting process. Since the ore dock at Escanaba is of timber construction, the hot pellets could present a fire hazard. The C&NW has set up a heat sensing device to determine the temperature of the pellets before the cars are placed on the dock for unloading. If a block of cars are too hot for unloading, they've set aside until the pellets have cooled for safe unloading.

Even though the C&NW dock is located on Lake Michigan with a milder climate than at Marquette on Lake Superior—just 60 miles to the North—the C&NW must still combat frozen ore in the Spring and Fall. To meet this challenge, the company has set up an infrared thawing shed at the ore yard. The difference between this facility and the DM&IR's facility at Two Harbors is that the C&NW installation uses electricity for power while the DM&IR

uses gas. Prior to this installation, the C&NW used two streamlined Hudsons, which once handled the Challengers and other Union Pacific passenger trains betwen Chicago and Omaha, for thawing frozen ore.

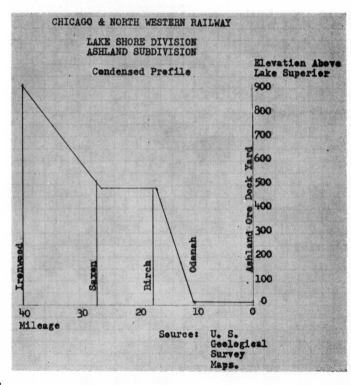

96

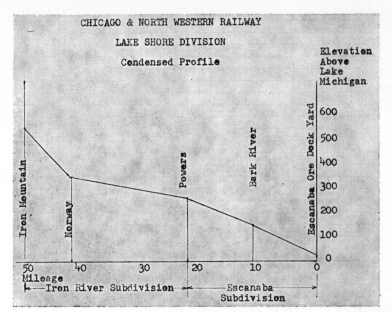

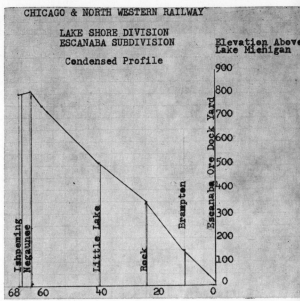

Passenger service is still operated in the ore territory. The Bi-level Peninsula 400 skirts the territory by joining the ore area at Powers to Escanaba. The Peninsula is the last year round passenger train operating to the Upper Peninsula. The only other passenger train to this part of the country is the Peninsula 400's companion train, the Flambeau 400. However, this train operates only during the Summer season and runs to Ironwood, Michigan.

The Milwaukee Road services the Champion Mine on the Marquette Range along with the Soo Line. The Milwaukee Road yard at Champion has four tracks. This is primarily a connection with the Soo Line for regular freight. Ore cars are handled on the tri-weekly freights No. 69 and 82, which operate between Channing and Champion. This is known as the Ninth Subdivision of the Milwaukee Division.

The Menominee Iron Range Ore Pooling Agreement is the largest ore operation of the C&NW and the Milwaukee Road. The pool is a rather unusual operation but it has given the two lines an efficient operation that would otherwise have been possible only through a merger. The two lines were not ready to merge yet in the 1930's, and this was the best solution to one of the many problems of the depression.

The Marquette Iron Range Operation

The C&NW also serves the Marquette Iron Range, but not with a pool agreement with the Milwaukee Road or any other railroad. The road's operations to Ishpeming are rather small compared to the Menominee Operation, but

nevertheless extremely important to the cash register. The C&NW operates one ore train per day from Escanaba to Ishpeming on a turn around basis. The train usually has 4 1600 HP F-M Roadswitchers and anywhere from 80 to 125 cars. The train shares this section of the Escanaba Subdivision with trains 209 and 214, the Peninsula 400 and trains 39 and 34, daily except Saturday freights. The ore extra runs on a daily basis. Often, there might be an extra freight train for logs on the line. The ore extra to Ishpeming usually has only North Western power, but if there are not enough units to go around one may see one or two Milwaukee units in the consist. No Milwaukee Road ore cars are used in the Marquette Iron Range operation.

The operation on this end of the railroad is fairly simple. The C&NW does not service any mines in the area. The Lake Superior & Ishpeming Railroad does all the switching and making up of ore train for the C&NW.

The ore trains arrive at Ishpeming on the new SOO-C&NW-LS&I joint main line. The train rolls into the new joint yard, and the caboose is cut off the train on the fly in front of the depot. The crew yards their train and returns to the depot to eat lunch.

If the ore extra is late, the LS&I power will be waiting for the train to arrive. When this occurs, the North Western crew drops the train on the main line and the engine goes into the yard. The LS&I locomotive will then back down and pick up the train and depart for the Western end of the Marquette Iron Range.

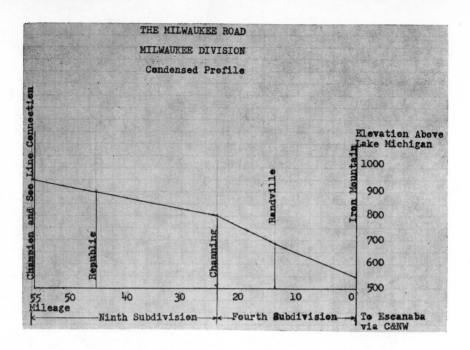

THE MILWAUKEE ROAD

MILWAUKEE DIVISION

Condensed Profile

After the crew has eaten their lunch, they pick up their caboose and place it on the end of a loaded ore train the LS&I has assembled. They build up their air, test the brakes and depart for Escanaba.

The Marquette Iron Range is the smallest of the ore operations on the North Western. The Railway handles the smallest amount of tonnage of the three railroads that serve the Marquette Iron Range. Even with the small operation, it is very much a thrill to see four units struggling to get their loaded 100 car train up the grade east of the Ishpeming Depot.

The Gogebic Iron Range Operation

Although the Gogebic Iron Range is no longer producing iron ore, it bears mentioning because it was once a substantial ore producing area. The production of the Range declined steadily from the 1920's. During that time over 9 million tons of ore per year were shipped through the Soo Line ore dock and the three C&NW ore docks at Ashland, Wisconsin. The year 1965 saw the last mine close and was the last year of ore shipping for the City of Ashland.

For most of the life of the Gogebic Range, the C&NW shipped the ore out of the port of Ashland. Ore was mined from Wakefield, Michigan to Montreal, Wisconsin. Ironwood, Michigan, situated in between these two points, had most of the mines and was the ore train assembly yard for the North Western. During the years up through 1960, there was considerable

traffic from the Gogebic Range, even though the amount of ore dwindled from 9 million tons to less than 3 million in those last "good" years.

The C&NW had a pool agreement with the Soo Line for ore hauling similar to the agreement with the Milwaukee Road. The C&NW moved 69% of the ore, while the Soo handled 31% of all the ore between the Gogebic Range and Ashland, Wisconsin. The roads used each other's tracks between Hoyt, Wisconsin and Wakefield, Michigan. For many years, they mixed their cars together but in the last few years the cars remained with their owners only. Up until the 1950's, the equipment was 50 ton ore cars only. As C&NW purchased more 70 ton cars from Bethlehem Steel Company, 70 ton cars began showing up in Ashland on the C&NW only. The Soo could not use these cars because of clearance problems at some of the mines on their trackage.

During the 40's and 50's, the operations of the C&NW were quite interesting. Empty trains were made up in the Ashland Ore Yard and the crew made a round trip between Ashland and Ironwood. The distance between Ashland and Ironwood is 40 miles. At Ironwood, the loaded trains were made up by the mine run assignments. Power used on mine run assignments in those days varied from Type R-1, 4-6-0's; and 1,000 HP Alco switchers to GP-7's.

The road crew upon their arrival in Ironwood would set out their train, eat lunch, and prepare to make the return run to Ashland.

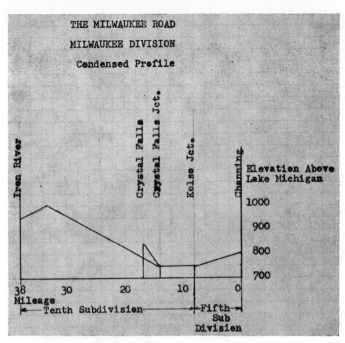

THE MILWAUKEE ROAD
MILWAUKEE DIVISION
Condensed Profile

Road power, after the 2-8-2's and 2-8-4's was 3 F-7's. The C&NW usually ran about 125 to 150 car trains. The car factor was 50 cars to each F-7. In the late 50's, when only one ore train per day was operating to Ironwood, four F-7's were put together for trains up to 180 cars. Steam power used to handle 80 to 90 cars and up to six crews per day used to operate to Ironwood for ore.

Upon arrival at Ashland, the crew would yard their train on one of two scale tracks. The power would be cut off and go to the roundhouse. The yard power would then weigh the train and classify the ore. After sorting, the cars of ore were stored until called for by the dock agent.

The ore dock operations at Ashland were quite interesting and fascinating. Originally, in the 20's and 30's, the C&NW owned three ore docks in Ashland. They were known as the No. 1, 2 and 3. In 1936, the No. 1 ore dock burned. It was a disaster not only for the railroad, but for the various fire departments that fought the blaze. The fire occurred in the dead of winter. The trucks went out on to the ice to fight the fire. The ice on top melted and the trucks were in several inches of water. Finally as the fire was put out and the temperature dropped, the trucks were frozen solid into Lake Superior.

The No. 1 dock was approximately half as long as the No. 2 and 3 ore docks. The No. 2 and 3 were identical in length and in capacity. They had 340 pockets and were 2,040 feet long.

The No. 2 was dismantled in 1948, when the C&NW saw that if some of the Gogebic Ore could be shipped through Escanaba, they could get along with only one ore dock in Ashland. The late 1940's saw about 4 million tons per year going through Ashland. The C&NW began to handle about 1 million of those tons to Escanaba in 1948 when the No. 2 was dismantled.

The C&NW used the No. 3 ore dock until 1957, when they began using the Soo Line ore dock. The No. 3 ore dock was dismantled in 1960. The pilings for this last dock can still be seen in the lake front.

When the C&NW operated their own ore docks, they used both steam type R-1's and 1000 HP Alco switchers. These engines could handle about 20 to 30 car shoves on their docks. The grade was slight and larger power was not needed. It was quite a sight to see ore stained ten wheelers shoving ore cars on to the timber ore docks.

In 1957, it was decided that it would be more economical to ship ore through the Soo Line ore dock. The Soo dock had considerable unused shipping capacity, so why have two docks operating when one could do the job. So an agreement was reached between the two roads, and the 1957 season saw C&NW GP-9's shoving 50 and 60 car cuts on the Soo ore dock. The Soo Line dock was quite busy for about 3 years with both roads handling about 3 million tons of ore per year through the dock.

North Western ore going through the Soo dock was not entirely a new operation. For some time after the No. 2 ore dock had been dismantled, the C&NW leased about 60 pockets on the Soo dock. The C&NW operated on the Soo dock during the third trick, when Soo operations were at a minimum or none at all.

In 1960, the far sighted North Western management recognized that the mining costs were going up, and if transportation costs or rates were not lowered, the mines on the Gogebic Range would stop operating very quickly. A study was made, and a decision to suspend operations at Ashland and transfer all C&NW ore to Escanaba was made. This decision actually forestalled the closing of many mines. The freight rate on iron ore to Escanaba was lowered, and the steel companies found that the faster turn-around by vessels also reduced their costs. Escanaba is much closer to the steel producing areas.

By 1960, all EMD F-7's were beginning to be removed from freight service and rebuilt for

HERE A FORD and an Interlake Steamship Company vessel prepare for loading at the No. 6 ore dock in Escanaba.—*Courtesy C&NW Ry.*

commuter streamliner service. Thus, this is the reason only F-M units are now seen in the ore country. F-M's were used to handle the ore to Ashland in 1959 and later to Escanaba.

It is extremely doubtful that the C&NW will ever use Ashland as an ore shipping port again. If a new pellet plant is built in the Iron-wood area, it would not make sense to back haul the ore to Ashland before it is shipped eastbound to the mills. If ore were to be discovered southwest of Ashland along the line to St. Paul, even that ore might be moved to Escanaba, unless it went by an all-rail route.

The Future

With new and the expanson of present pellet plants on the Marquette and Menominee Iron Ranges, the ore traffic on the C&NW-Milwaukee Road looks very healthy. The Roads have been working to keep the ranges competitive with foreign ores by lower freight rates, by rebuilding ore cars for greater capacity, and by building a new ore dock at Escanaba. With the two companies providing the mining companies with sound, inexpensive and efficient transportation tools, the future looks very bright indeed.

ANOTHER VIEW of the Ford and Interlake being loaded. Note the rebuilt ore cars with extensions being shoved onto the ore dock. These cars are assigned to hauling pellets.—*Courtesy C&NW Ry.*

HERE CHUTES of the North Western ore dock at Escanaba are lowered into the hold of an ore vessel. —*Courtesy C&NW Ry.*

A VIEW of the old No. 5 before dismantling. There were once 4 ore docks in Escanaba, now only one. The Soo Line once owned and operated an ore dock in Gladstone, a town only a few miles from Escanaba.—*Courtesy C&NW Ry.*

AN ARTIST'S CONCEPT of the new ore dock presently under construction at the City of Escanaba. Note the automatic train positioner and the fact that the dock is very low. Quite a contrast to the 80 foot high structures that were still being built as late as 1946.—*Courtesy C&NW Ry.*

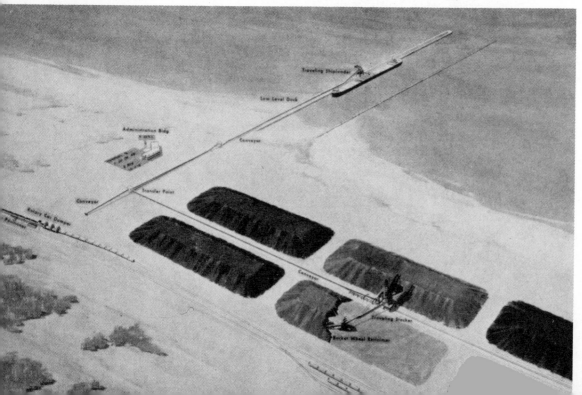

A **VIEW** of the thawing plant at Escanaba. One can almost feel the heat.—*Courtesy C&NW Ry.*

AERIAL VIEWS of the C&NW dock at Escanaba. One can see where the No. 5 used to stand.

THIS MACHINE is called a bucket wheel reclaimer. It digs into the piles of ore and pellets and places the raw material onto the belt that transports it out on the dock and into the ship's hold.—*Courtesy C&NW Ry.*

THIS IS THE MACHINE that will pile the iron ore and pellets after unloading from the train.— *Courtesy C&NW Ry.*

THESE TWO TYPES of steam power were the most frequently used on the old Ashland and Peninsula Division ore trains just prior to dieselization. These two divisions have since been merged into the Lake Shore Division.—*Courtesy C&NW Ry.*

THE MILWAUKEE ROAD contributed 2-8-2's to the ore pool before dieselization. When diesels came in, the Milwaukee Road also sent 1600 HP Fairbanks-Morse power to the ore district.

THE C&NW operates Fairbanks, Morse & Company 1600 HP Road-switchers in both yard and road service in the ore territory.—*Courtesy Fairbanks, Morse & Co.*

1600 H.P. D.E. LOCOMOTIVE (LD-197) CHICAGO & NORTH WESTERN R.R.
F.EF.   FAIRBANKS, MORSE & CO.   8991R

A TOP VIEW of the last timber ore dock at Escanaba.—*Courtesy C&NW Ry.*

FAIRBANKS-MORSE power replaced Electro-Motive Division F-7 units in ore service when the "F" units were rebuilt for Chicago area passenger service. This unit is an early model 1600 HP Road-switcher.—*Courtesy Fairbanks, Morse & Co.*

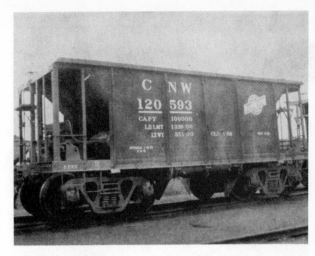

50 TON ORE CARS before and after rebuilding.

THE C&NW has had a shortage of ore cars in recent years, and so purchased 1,000 of them from the DM&IR. This is one of the 50 ton cars purchased that was rebuilt with an extension for pellet service.

A BUILDER'S PHOTO of the C&NW 70 ton ore car.—*Courtesy Bethlehem Steel Company*

A REBUILT Milwaukee Road ore car. These cars are used in the pool service with the CNW.

A BUILDER'S PHOTO of the type caboose used on the ore runs. —*Courtesy Thrall Car Co.*

THE C&NW has rebuilt part of its ore car fleet to handle iron ore pellets. Pellets weigh less per cubic foot than does iron ore. Therefore, extensions are placed on ore cars in order for them to carry a 70 ton payload.

THE MILWAUKEE ROAD maintains a 4 track yard at Champion for connection with the Soo Line. On the day this photo was taken, there were only 4 cars of Champion Mine ore in the yard. The pulpwood in the background is enroute to Green Bay paper mills.

Chapter Six

Soo Line Railroad
Ore Operations
Marquette and Ashland

THE SOO LINE RAILROAD was a unique ore hauler until the year 1966, in that it shipped ore through three different ports: Superior, Ashland and Marquette. The latter port was through the merger with the Duluth, South Shore & Atlantic Railway. The Soo also used to ship iron ore through Gladston, Michigan. This operation, along with the 768 foot long ore dock, was discontinued early in the 20th Century.

The Soo's iron ore operations can be broken into three categories according to port. This writer will cover the Marquette and Ashland operations in this chapter, and the Superior Operation in the chapter on the Cuyuna Range. The three operations have always been separate and never linked with each other in any way.

The Marquette operation is the smallest ore operation in Michigan, but nevertheless is very exciting. The operations are divided up into three categories, the ore yard and dock, the road and the mine run.

The Soo serves two mines on the Marquette Iron Range, the Tracy at Negaunee and the Champion at Champion. The latter ore is a hematite and is blue-gray in color. It is shipped either in a lump form or crushed and is usually not mixed with any other ores. The road ore trains serve this mine directly, as the mine run assignments do not travel as far as Champion. The Tracy mine is served by the mine run assignments. There may be one or two of these assignments per day in the Negaunee area. Frequently, the regular switching assignment handles the mine assignments depending upon the level of business. The cars of Tracy ore are brought to the Hogan Ore Yard for the ore extras.

The road ore trains are handled in a turn around type of assignment between Marquette and Hogan Ore Yard or Marquette and Champion. Crews called for Hogan Ore Yard turns make two round trips between Marquette and Hogan. This is the same type of arrangment found on the LS&I. There is usually only one crew per day on the Hogan Ore Yard turns, but two crews are not uncommon and as many as four have been called in one 24 hour period. Crews called for the Champion run make only a single round trip.

The ore trains operated in this territory of 30 miles between Marquette and Champion, are the shortest operated anywhere in the Lake Superior Region. This writer has seen trains as short as 44 cars. Assistant Trainmaster Charles Francisco at Marquette stated that trains have been as short as 30, but the normal length is 60 cars. The power used on the road trains is usually 2 EMD GP-9's or 2 Baldwin 1,600 HP C + C Road Switchers. The latter power is rapidly being scrapped by the Soo Line and will soon no longer be seen in Marquette Iron Range service.

The operations of the ore trains in this territory are not too different from the operations of other railroad ore trains. The loaded trains are limited to 25 MPH and 30 MPH for the empties. This rule also applies to freight trains handling ore cars.

Before the ore trains depart Hogan Ore Yard, all the retainers are set in the high pressure position because of the 2% to 2.67% descending grade between Mile Post 160.5 and the

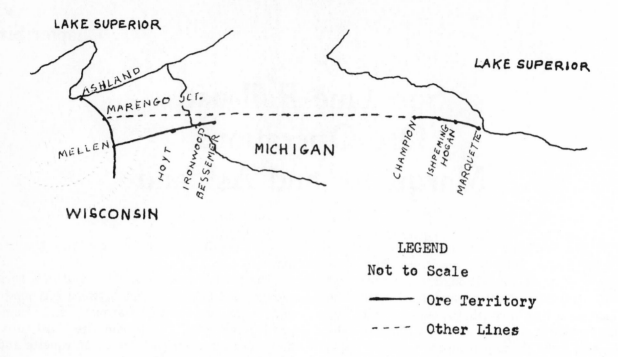

LAKE SUPERIOR

ASHLAND

MARENGO JCT.

MELLEN

HOYT

IRONWOOD

BESSEMER

MICHIGAN

WISCONSIN

LAKE SUPERIOR

CHAMPION

ISHPEMING HOGAN

MARQUETTE

LEGEND

Not to Scale

——— Ore Territory

- - - - Other Lines

ore dock yard. The loaded trains are limited to 15 MPH from MP 160.5 to the ore dock yard. By the time the trains arrive at the Highway 41 over pass before entering the ore dock yard, the entire train is nearly hidden from view because of the blue smoke from the brakes, a scene not unlike the DM&IR's Proctor Hill show of blue smoke.   Upon arrival at the West Switch of the yard, the train must come to a complete stop before entering the yard itself. After stopping for the switch to the receiving yard, the engineer then releases the train brakes and holds the train with the engine brake. The rear brakeman then lets down retainers starting from the rear of the train. On 40 or more cars, 20 retainers are let down; 30 to 40 cars, 15 retainers must be let down; less than 30 cars, not less than 50% of the retainer may be let down. No retainers can be let down on the head end of the train to prevent the train from getting out of control while going into the yard. It is quite a sight to see a loaded ore train arriving at the Marquette Ore Dock Yard.

The ore dock and yard operations are very unique in that the Soo uses both its ore yard, which is situated west of the dock; and its freight yard, which is situated along the lake front, for the switching or storing of ore before

its placement on the dock. The ore yard is used for Soo ore and LS&I ore. The freight yard is used for LS&I ore when the ore yard is plugged. With the increasing ore shipments off the Mar-

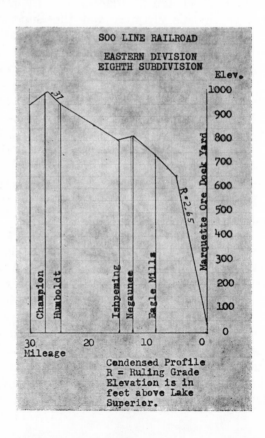

SOO LINE RAILROAD

EASTERN DIVISION
EIGHTH SUBDIVISION

Elev.

Champion

Humboldt

Ishpeming

Negaunee

Eagle Mills

Marquette Ore Dock Yard

Mileage

Condensed Profile
R = Ruling Grade
Elevation is in feet above Lake Superior.

112

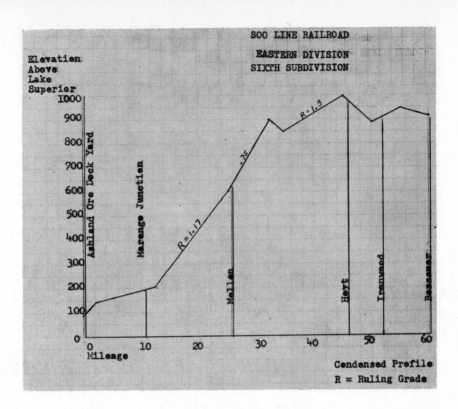

Condensed Profile
R = Ruling Grade

quette Range, the ore yard is frequently plugged.

Normally, with a little more than 1 million tons of ore per year shipped over the Marquette dock; the Soo uses just one engine crew on the ore dock per day. This crew does all the weighing, dock shoving, sorting of ore cars and the making up of the road trains for the Marquette Range. The ore dock is of concrete construction, 900 feet long and has a capacity of 56,000 tons. The approach is of steel and timber construction with a maximum grade of less than 1%.

Early in the morning, just west of the Marquette Passenger Station, one can see two empty ore trains assembled complete with caboose and awaiting motive power and crew. These are the trains for Hogan Ore Yard. If a Champion run is going to be made, it is made up after the departure of the first Hogan Turn. In the early evening, one can see two loaded trains from Hogan in the receiving yard just east of the Highway 41 over pass. Often, the Champion Turn will have arrived and three trains can be seen, two with the Tracy red ore and one with the Champion blue ore.

On any given day, if there is to be only Soo Line ore to be sorted, weighed and spotted on the dock, only one 1600 HP Baldwin Road Switcher or a GP-9 is used. The single unit can push at least 40 cars up the approach to the

dock. There is a 10 MPH speed limit on the approach and the ore dock.

If there is interchange ore with the LS&I, the dock motive power requirements are a different story. The LS&I delivers ore to the Soo Line at the Soo freight yard. There is a steep grade between the freight yard and the ore yard. The dock crew must take the ore from the freight yard to the ore yard in order to shove onto the dock. Two units are used for this operation. The two units can handle only about 2,000 tons out of the freight yard. Most of the LS&I ore cars are 75 ton capacity and 95 ton capacity. This means that the two units will be truly struggling, wide open, with only 20 to 25 ore cars.

Tracy ore is a soft sticky ore. It is rather difficult to get out of the ore cars on the ore dock. Once in the pocket, the ore is again reluctant to flow freely into the boats. To aid this problem on the ore dock is a unique switching arrangement. A car of pellets is placed into the pocket first. Then the Tracy ore is dumped on top of it. When the chute is lowered into a boat, the pellets flow freely and there is no base for the Tracy to rest on, so it falls out too, quite fast—the ore punchers hope!

The Marquette Iron Range is healthy and prosperous. The Soo has had increases in annual tonnages over their dock during the last few years. Although these increases have been small, amounting to about 100,000 tons or so per year, they are significant in view of the general decline of ore shipments from other ranges because of the importing of ores from foreign countries.

The Ashland Operations

The ore operations at Ashland came to an unfortunate end in August, 1965. During that month, the Soo loaded its last boat load of Gogebic Range iron ore—stockpiled from the second last operating mine—the Cary at Montreal, Wisconsin. In 1965, less than 600,000 tons of ore were shipped through the Ashland port. This amount, as compared to some of the 1920's totals of nearly nine million tons going over four ore docks, is very sad indeed. (The Soo owned one of the four ore docks, the C& NW the other three.)

In the last good years, say 1950 to 1960, the Soo shipped around one to one and one half million tons per year. The Soo Line had a mine transfer engine that operated between Hoyt, Wisconsin and Bessemer, Michigan; a distance of 13.4 miles. The loads were collected either from the mines or from the C&NW and taken to Hoyt. At Hoyt, loaded trains were made up for the trip to Ashland.

Road crews operated out of Ashland. Crews for ore extras were usually called in the early evening, and the ore train would follow the old time freight for Chicago out of town. Trains of 125 cars were common and the trip took from 6 to 10 hours. Motive power was usually 2 1500 HP Road Alcos, or 2 F-7's, or 2 GP-9's. Sometimes, when a train was light, only one GP-9 was used.

One other train handled a substantial, in fact, most of the ore between the Range and Ashland. This was the local between Ashland and Bessemer, Nos. 51 and 52. No. 52 went to work about 6:30 AM at Ashland. It had three

THE SOO LINE ore dock at Marquette, Michigan. The ore dock is 900 feet long and has a storage capacity of 56,000 tons.

THE SOO'S 1800 FOOT ORE DOCK at Ashland. When it was built in 1916, it was the largest concrete ore dock in the world. It was often used in speed loading races with the DM&IR No. I ore dock in Two Harbors. No one was ever quite sure which dock was the fastest loader until the DM&IR dock was rebuilt with wider chutes and doors.

units and handled up to 135 ore cars, plus any local freight there might have been. It normally took about 12 hours for the train to make its trip to Bessemer and return. This train was a mixed train for many years and carried a combine on the rear. To my knowledge, this ore train was the only one in the country that could carry passengers. It was rather amusing to see 3 units, 125 ore cars and a combine. The Soo Line maroon combine was even redder from the iron ore.

In the days of steam, the Soo used 2-8-2's, which handled 125 cars alone with ease and pomp.

The ore dock yard has one long receiving track. The ore trains pulled in on this track. The switch engines then pulled the train, about 40 cars at a time, over the scale and down into a classification track. The cars were ordered to the dock by the ore dock agent as they were needed for boat loading.

The Soo Line used four types of power on the Ashland dock: 1000 HP Alco switchers and road switchers, which were limited to 35 car shoves; 1200 HP EMD switchers, which had 40 car limits; and 1750 HP EMD GP-9's, which had 45 car limits. These limits were set up for the sole purpose of preventing the trains from stalling on the approach to the ore dock. During the days of steam, the Soo assigned a 2-10-0 to work the Ashland dock. This engine is on permanent display next to the ore dock approach on U. S. Highway 2 in Ashland. This engine pushed 37 cars up to the dock.

During World War II, a 2-8-0 was used as a helper engine on the ore dock. This was quite an operation. A shove of 70 cars or more would be made up in the ore yard. The 2-10-0 or a 2-8-0 would couple up to the long shove. Then the helper engine would also couple on to the front of the shove engine. The two steam engines would then work very hard shoving the

long train of ore up the approach. As the steamers rolled over the Second Street Bridge, the helper would cut off and drift back down to the ore yard, where it would make up the next shove for the ore dock.

The ore dock in Ashland is of concrete construction. It is 1800 feet long and has a 105,000 ton capacity. The approach to the ore dock is built of timber with a short section of concrete just before the dock itself.

The ore cars used in Ashland were of the 50 ton variety. Seventy-five ton cars were tried, but could not fit under some of the mine loading spouts, and because the mines were becoming more expensive to operate and would eventually close, the Soo never purchased 75 ton equipment for use on the Gogebic Range.

Future ore operations in Ashland depend fully on the development of taconite pellet plants. It has been rumored for years that one would be built in the Park Falls area, but nothing has ever been announced. At the present time, the Ashland ore dock, ore yard and other facilities are idle. This is a very sad sight, indeed.

However, there are millions of tons of taconite on the Eastern End of the Gogebic Range. It might be considered a good investment to build a plant on the eastern end of the Gogebic because the Soo Line has the transportation facilities available for immediate use. When the needs of the steel mills require a plant for pellet production be built on the Gogebic, the men of the Soo's Eastern Division will be willing, ready and able to handle the new tonnage.

LOOKING NORTH into the ore classification yard at Ashland. This picture was taken in 1962 before the last mine closed on the Gogebic Range. If one were to visit this yard now, he would find the yard full of stored cars, cars that are condemned, and often brand new cars awaiting final inspection before going into service.

THIS VIEW shows the Hoyt Yard in 1960. Ore extras to the Gogebic Range arrived and departed from this yard near Montreal, Wisconsin.—*Courtesy Soo Line*

THIS STEAM LOCOMOTIVE was used for several years at Ashland and later at Marquette for thawing frozen ore and slushing service on the ore docks. The tank ahead of the 2449 was used for an additional water supply.

THE USUAL SWITCHING POWER for the Ashland ore dock was a 1200 HP diesel switcher. Here the 2112, an ex-Wisconsin Central unit, switches the south lead.

GP-9'S WERE OFTEN ASSIGNED to ore dock service in Ashland. Here the 413 awaits its crew and the 7:30 a.m. time to go to work. This engine was capable of pushing 50 fifty ton ore cars up the grade and onto the dock.

THE WISCONSIN CENTRAL, Soo Line and the DSS&A all invested in this Pullman Standard sloped end ore car. To this writer's knowledge, no other road purchased this type of car. Note the WC in the left hand corner indicating the car was owned by the Wisconsin Central.

A 50 TON ORE CAR used by the Soo at Superior and Ashland, and later on at Marquette.

AN EX-DSS&A ORE CAR on the rip track at Marquette for repairs. If the reader will compare this picture with one of the C&NW ore cars, he will notice that they are nearly identical.

Chapter Seven

The Cuyuna Range Railroads

THE CUYUNA IRON RANGE mines are served by the Northern Pacific and the Soo Line in a joint operating pool agreement. The roads have jointly served the Cuyuna with the ore pool since April 15, 1929. The ore mined on the Cuyuna Range is shipped on a 50-50 basis over the two railroads to the Northern Pacific ore dock in Superior.

The two railroads handle the ore between Ironton, Minnesota and Superior, Wisconsin. The NP operates 99.4 miles of ore district between their Hill Avenue Ore Yard in Superior and Ironton. Soo Line Road ore trains arrive and depart from the NP Hill Avenue Yard, but use their own line between Superior and McGregor. Between McGregor and Ironton, the Soo has trackage rights over the Northern Pacific. The total mileage for the Soo's ore district is 105.3 miles.

The two companies maintain three yards for the movement of iron ore. The Hill Avenue Yard in Superior is used for weighing, ore classification and storage until the cars are shoved onto the ore dock for dumping. The Old Yard at Ironton is used as an arrival yard for empties, and the New Yard at Ironton is used as a departure yard for loads.

The Ore Pool arrangement was set up in the Spring of 1929 for the primary purpose of improved customer service and reducing expenses at the same time. The Pool arrangement permitted the two railroads to remove duplicate trackage on the Cuyuna Range, and allowed the Soo Line to discontinue operations and the dismantling of a timber ore dock and ore yard at Superior. Ore cars are pooled on a tonnage capacity basis. Each railroad furnishes the same proportion of the total car tonnage capacity required throughout the year.

Each railroad provides an equal amount of locomotives and crews for service to the mines on the Range. At Superior, the NP furnishes the power for the ore yard and dock while the Soo provides crews for the dock switching for half of the switching hours at the Hill Avenue Yard.

The agreement provides that the NP appoints an Ore Superintendent—subject to approval by the Soo—who is in charge of all pool operations for both lines on the Range, yards and on the dock in Superior. The Soo Line in turn appoints a Trainmaster at Ironton, subject to approval by the Northern Pacific. The Trainmaster supervises operations on the Range and reports directly to the Ore Superintendent.

With this type of a pool agreement, the NP and the Soo were able to handle smoothly and efficiently approximately one to three million tons of ore per year between the Range and the ore dock. (However in 1967, a major mine closed and the 1968 shipments will be considerably less than 1 million tons of ore.) These operations can be placed in three categories, the Range operations, the Road haul, and the ore dock operations. These operations, because of the pool, are somewhat different from other railroad iron ore operations.

Cuyuna Range Switching Operations

The mine service operations on the NP and the Soo at Ironton are divided up evenly. Both the Soo and the NP maintain one locomotive and crew each for the range operations. Each railroad operates its crew and motive power during the day shift. If an afternoon crew is needed, the roads trade off that operation making sure that the switching hours on the Range are divided upon a 50-50 basis. The Soo normally operates a 1500 HP Baldwin Roadswitch-

NORTHERN PACIFIC RAILWAY

and

SOO LINE RAILROAD

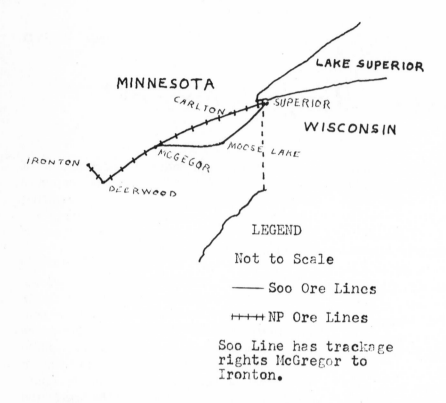

LEGEND

Not to Scale

—— Soo Ore Lines

++++ NP Ore Lines

Soo Line has trackage
rights McGregor to
Ironton.

er on Range, and the NP has either a GP-9 or an Alco 1800 HP Roadswitcher.

The crews service all mines and industries of the Ironton area. The empty ore cars are distributed from the Old Yard to the various mines. The loads are brought to the New Yard. Road ore extras arrive at the Old Yard and depart from the New Yard. The Range crews have the responsibility for breaking up and assembling of ore trains.

In addition, the crews handle ore from Ironton to Deerwood. The NP handles most of their ore in regular freight trains. The trains, such as No. 623 and 624 to and from Staples, set out empties and pick up loads for Superior at Deerwood. The range crews have the responsibility to pick up the empty ore cars and to deliver the loads to the Deerwood Yard.

Both Railroads' crews operate between Deerwood and Ironton, a distance of 3.9 miles and NP trackage. The crews make frequent trips between the two points hauling ore for the Superior dock, ore for all rail shipment to either the Chicago or St. Louis area steel mills

and miscellaneous freight. Therefore, the two crews must be watchful of each other's movements, and be on the lookout for road trains on the NP's main line to Staples and ore extras arriving and departing Ironton.

Road Operations

During the last few years, the volume of ore shipped over the ore dock has only been about 1 million tons annually. Therefore, ore extras are somewhat rare between Superior and Ironton, particularly on the NP. For the most part, the NP handles their volume of ore in their road trains. Freight trains No. 623 and 624, which run between Duluth and Staples, operate via the Central Avenue Yard in Superior to handle the ore business. The ore dock crews handle the empties and loads between Hill Avenue ore dock yard and the Central Avenue Yard. No. 623 picks up empties at Central Avenue and then continues on to Staples, dropping the empty ore cars at Deerwood. The speed limit for trains handling empty ore cars is 40 MPH.

120

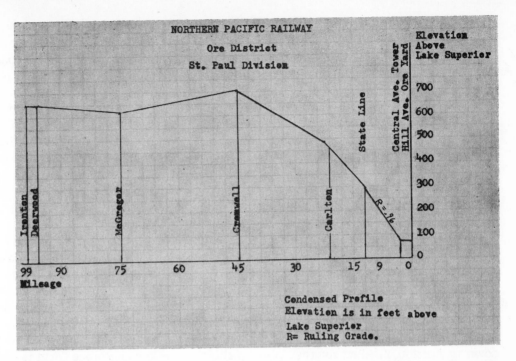

NORTHERN PACIFIC RAILWAY
Ore District
St. Paul Division

Condensed Profile
Elevation is in feet above
Lake Superior
R= Ruling Grade.

Eastward freight trains enroute to Duluth, which contain loaded ore cars, travel via Central Avenue Superior otherwise the eastward freight trains operate via West Duluth into the Duluth Yard.

When the NP operates ore extras, the trains are usually assigned 3 units, made up of a combination of EMD GP-9's and/or Alco 1500 HP or 1800 HP road switchers. Train lengths run up to 220 cars. These trains make a turn around run between the Superior Ore yard and Ironton. Ore extras on the NP usually take about 12 hours to complete a turn around run.

The Soo Line operates most of the ore extras operated by the two roads between Superior and Ironton. The principal reason for this is that Ironton is located away from the main line, and it would be difficult for trains operating between Superior and Federal Dam to move down to Ironton from McGregor to pick up loads and leave empties. This operation would have a tendency to be irregular, and could cause

ORE EXTRAS on the Central Division arrive and depart from the NP's Hill Avenue yard. Here 2 GP-9's and a GP-30 prepare to depart for Ironton with 185 empties

a shortage of empties for loading at the mines. Therefore, the Soo finds it much easier and more economical to run an ore extra once or twice a week for its portion of the tonnage shipped over the Superior ore dock.

Ore trains on the Soo Line are quite interesting because of their two railroad operation, grades encountered with the loaded ore trains, and because the trains are among the heaviest operated anywhere in the world. Let's take a look at a typical Soo Line ore extra.

As stated previously, the Soo usually runs about one ore extra per week. Most of the time, the crew is called before noon time when an ore extra is run. Power for the trains vary. GP-30's and 35's in groups of two are sometimes used. Most of the time, however, three unit combinations of F-7's and GP-9's supply the power.

The crew picks up their engine at the 21st Street Roundhouse in Superior. They move down to Stinson Yard where they pick up their orders and caboose. From there, they roll across Stinson Avenue and switch over to the Northern Pacific Main Line. They back into the yard, run around their empty train and place the caboose on the train. They return to the head end of the train, couple on and begin pumping up the air. After the brakes have been tested, and the train given its final inspection, the train departs the Northern Pacific Hill Avenue Yard and crosses back on to the Soo Line

Main Line out of Stinson Yard. Empty trains usually have about 200 cars.

After the train has crossed over from the NP to the Soo, it enters 3.5 miles of Rule 261 Territory. (Rule 261 states, "On portions of the railroad, and on designated tracks so specified in the timetable, trains will be governed by block signals, whose indications will supersede the superiority of trains for both opposing and following movements on the same track.") At the end of this territory is Junction 278, where the Minneapolis line and the Thief River Falls line split.

The ore train continues down the Thief River Falls line to McGregor. At McGregor, the ore extra turns off the Soo and on to the Northern Pacific's main line to Staples. Orders and clearance form are also picked up at McGregor for the Authority to run over the NP. The train continues on to Deerwood, where another clearance form is picked up for authority to run from Deerwood to Ironton. Ironton is about 3 miles off the main line from Deerwood.

Upon arrival at Deerwood, the road crew must be constantly on the look out for the Range Assignments, which could be switching at either Deerwood or at the east end of the New Yard at Ironton.

The road crew normally takes the empty ore cars directly to the Old Yard. The crew then ties up and eats lunch.

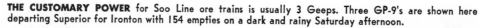

THE CUSTOMARY POWER for Soo Line ore trains is usually 3 Geeps. Three GP-9's are shown here departing Superior for Ironton with 154 empties on a dark and rainy Saturday afternoon.

BOTH THE NORTHERN PACIFIC and the Soo Line use road switchers for serving the mines on the Cuyuna Range. This unit is awaiting orders for an overtime assignment.

After lunch, the crew places their caboose on the rear of the loaded ore train in the New Yard. They then have to double the train, build up the air, test the brakes and have the usual inspection before departing. The crew picks up a clearance form to run to Deerwood, and at Deerwood they pick up another clearance form and orders for running to McGregor.

At McGregor, they pick up another set of orders and clearance form for running over the Soo Line to Superior.

Upon arrival at Superior, the ore train crosses over to the NP main line and proceeds into the Hill Avenue Ore Yard. They stop at the scale house and turn in the bills to the Weighmaster. At that point, the road crew begins a very tedious job of weighing those ore cars at the very slow speed of 3 miles per hour. It takes about 1 hour and 15 minutes to weigh 200 cars of ore, the usual size of an ore train for the Soo.

It normally takes from 13 to 16 hours for a crew to make an Ironton Turn. It is not unusual for a crew to "die on the vine" as it is called, when a crew doesn't make it back within 16 hours. Then another crew has to be called and driven out to the ore train, wherever it might be, and relieve the original crew.

In the days of steam, the Soo used 2-8-2's on the ore extras and 125 car trains were the rule

of thumb. Ten and twenty years ago, when the tonnage was over 3 million per year, the Soo used to run one or two ore extras on a daily basis and the same amount for the NP. The reduction of the tonnage has resulted in a great decrease in the amount of ore trains to the Cuyuna Range.

After the Soo crew has completed weighing the train and it has been yarded, it is the duty of the yard crew to complete the responsibility of the transportation of the ore from Mine to Dock.

Superior Ore Dock and Yard Operations

The crews at the Hill Avenue Yard have five functions to perform: 1. The weighing and classification of ore. 2. Spotting the cars on the ore dock. 3. The assembly of Soo Line and NP ore extras. 4. The movement of interchange ore over to the Great Northern's Allouez Ore Yard. 5. The movement of empties and loads to and from Central Avenue for movement in trains 623 and 624 to and from Deerwood and Ironton. Interchange ore to and from the DM&IR is handled by a road crew known as the Pokey Turn. This crew operates out of Duluth and handles loads and empties to and from the DM &IR in the following manner. NP-Soo ore destined the DM&IR is brought from either the Hill Avenue Yard or Central Avenue Yard to

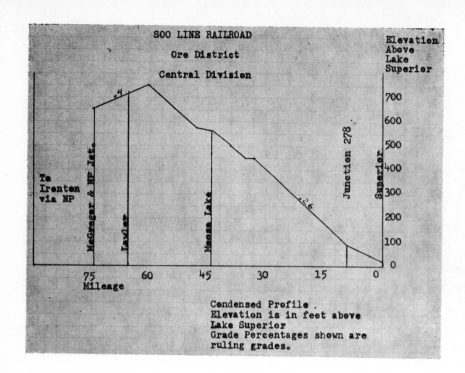

SOO LINE RAILROAD

Ore District

Central Division

Condensed Profile.
Elevation is in feet above
Lake Superior
Grade Percentages shown are
ruling grades.

Pokegama. Pokegama is the junction point for the NP and DM&IR on the DM&IR's Interstate Branch. Sometimes, No. 624 will set out ore destined for the DM&IR at Pokegama. DM&IR ore destined the NP dock is handled by the Pokey Turn between Pokegama and Central Avenue or Hill Avenue.

The ore dock crew usually begins its assignment by handling the ore set out by 624 the previous evening from Central Avenue to the Hill Avenue Yard. The first thing that must be done with the ore is to weigh it and perform the necessary classifying according to the mine and grade of ore. If the Soo Line had an ore extra the previous day, this ore need be classified only, as it was weighed upon the arrival of the train.

Upon completion of these duties, the crew may receive orders for certain cars that are to be spotted on the ore dock. The crew then assembles a train of up to 115 cars for shoving on to the ore dock. This is the longest shove of any Company's ore dock operations. To do this, NP and Soo Line crews use two unit NP roadswitchers, such GP-9's and Alco 1500 and 1800 HP road-switchers. After the cars are spotted on the dock, any empties that may be on the dock are gathered up and hauled back down to the yard.

If there is any interchange ore going to the Great Northern, the crew may get an order to take this ore over to the GN as their next assignment. The crew makes up the train of interchange ore and takes the ore directly to a small yard located on the east side of the Great Northern's classification yard in Allouez. If the GN has any ore destined the NP dock, they deliver directly to the NP yard.

Upon completion of dock and interchange duties, the ore dock crew may have one or two jobs left to complete. One is the making up of a Soo Line ore extra, if one is going to be run the next morning—or an NP ore extra if there is going to be one scheduled. The other is the assembly of empties for movement to the Central Avenue Yard for train No. 623 for movement to Deerwood and Ironton. When all duties at the Hill Avenue Yard are completed, the crew will take the empties to Central Avenue Yard as they return to the Roundhouse for the completion of their day's assignment.

The Northern Pacific no longer thaws ore during the late Fall when freezing weather occurs. The ore is sent directly over to the Great Northern Yard, thawed in their steam plant and placed on their docks for unloading. The NP once used steam locomotives for thawing, but as their expenses exceeded their worth for thawing purposes; the operation was discontinued entirely and transferred to the Great Northern Yard.

NORTHERN PACIFIC time freights No. 623 and 624 handle most of the NP ore traffic between Superior and the Cuyuna Range. A short while ago, No. 624 set out these loads in the Central Avenue yard (shown here). The loads will be picked up by the Hill Avenue yard crew for weighing, sorting and movement onto the ore dock.

The movement of the ore through the dock completes the responsibility of the NP and the Soo Line. This last operation puts the final touch on the work of the miners of the Cuyuna Range, the Mine Run switch crews at Ironton, the NP-Soo road crews, the yard and dock crews, agents, operators, dispatchers, Trainmasters, Traveling Engineers, Chief Dispatchers, the Division Superintendents and the Ore Superintendent in the movement of iron ore from underground to lake vessel.

HERE IS AN EARLY VIEW of the Northern Pacific ore dock. The photo was taken before the 1920's. The ore dock is still much the same today as it was then. The name of the ship in the photo is unknown. The ship is small compared to today's vessels. In this case, the vessel is only about 500 feet long.—Courtesy Northern Pacific

THIS IS THE NEW YARD at Ironton. This yard is used for assembling the ore extras for Superior.

THE NORTHERN PACIFIC DOCK is 1,860 feet long and has a 108,500 ton storage capacity. The dock was originally built in 1913 and was extended twice in 1917 and 1926. One can see the length of the first section of the dock by the differences in the alignment of the chutes.

A SOO LINE CREW uses two NP road switchers for switching empty ore cars from the ore dock at Hill Avenue yard in Superior.

THE SOO has a large fleet of tapered side ore cars in Minnesota. None of these have been used on the Michigan ranges even though the Soo purchased this type as early as the late 1920's.

THE SOO LINE has six different types of ore cars in service in Minnesota. This type, with a capacity of 75 tons, was the last group ordered by the Soo.

MOST ORE CARS stand idle during most of the winter season. However, some are pressed into coal service. In this case, the Northern Pacific is shoving several carloads of coal into a Duluth steam heating plant.

THE NORTHERN PACIFIC uses just one basic type of ore car. Here is one that was built in 1957 and is equipped with roller bearings.—*Courtesy Northern Pacific*

TWO HUNDRED 70 TON ore cars were built at Northern Pacific's Brainerd, Minnesota shops early in 1950.

THIS VIEW shows the completed train leaving Hillcrest. The train will run directly to Chicago, stopping only to change crews.—*Courtesy Soo Line*

A SOO LINE ore extra arriving at old yard in Ironton, Minnesota. The old yard is used as an arrival yard on the Cuyuna Iron Range.

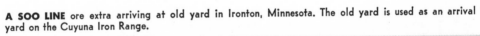

THE SOO LINE interchanges all-rail ore with the DM&IR at Ambridge, Wisconsin. Here an Eastern Division crew is picking up a train at that location. This train is enroute to Granite City, Ill. via the Soo to Chicago and the Norfolk and Western Railway beyond.—*Courtesy Soo Line*

NOT ALL SOO LINE all-rail ore comes from the DM&IR. This particular ore train was interchanged at Minneapolis from the Great Northern Railway. It is shown here departing Shoreham yard and is enroute to Chicago.—*Courtesy Soo Line*

THE NORTHERN PACIFIC and the Soo Line normally use two NP road switchers for the Superior ore dock service. Here 2 units are departing the Hill Avenue yard with 56 loads for the Great Northern's Allouez ore yard.

ALL RAIL ORE TRAINS enroute to Chicago must be doubled from Ambridge to Hillcrest because of a rather steep grade up from Superior. This photo was taken from the locomotive of an all rail ore train as it is arriving at Hillcrest with the second half of the train.—*Courtesy Soo Line*

Chapter Eight

Other Ore Carriers

THE CANADIAN NATIONAL is the large Ontario ore hauler that has a similar type of operation to that found in Minnesota and Michigan. The CN's ore operations extend from Port Arthur, Ontario to Atikokan, a distance of 141.4 miles.

The CN serves the Steep Rock Iron Range at Atikokan. The area loads some 3 million tons of raw iron ore and pellets per year into Canadian National ore cars. The operation is relatively new compared with the other ore operations. In fact, it began out of great need for iron ore during the Second World War. The ore was needed in such a hurry that there was no time to build an ore dock in Port Arthur. Consequently, during the war years and while the dock at Port Arthur was under construction, the ore was shipped over to Fort Frances. From that point, the ore moved via a CN subsidiary, the Duluth, Winnipeg and Pacific Railway to Duluth. After arrival in the West Duluth Yard, the ore was taken to Superior and shipped over the Great Northern Railway ore docks.

After the ore dock was completed in 1946, the Steep Rock Ore began moving to Port Arthur and through the last pocket ore dock to be built on the Great Lakes.

To handle the present ore traffic of approximately 3 million tons annually, the CN maintains a fleet of 85 ton ore cars and 62½ ton ore cars. More than 300 of the 85 ton cars have been fitted with extended sides for pellet service.

A switch crew is located at Atikokan for servicing the pellet plant and the mines, and for the making up and breaking up of trains.

Trains of empties are dispatched from Port Arthur to Atikokan. The ore trains are about 100 cars long and are handled by 3 or 4 unit diesel locomotives. Usually the power for the ore trains is either General Motors or Montreal Locomotive Works Road Switchers. The loaded trains are limited to 30 miles per hour and running time between Port Arthur and Atikokan is about 5 hours. Of all the ore operations in the Lake Superior District, the CN's is the only one that is not a turn around run. The crews are operated as a "chain gang" arrangement between Port Arthur and Atikokan. That is, the first crew that arrives is also the first crew to depart. A crew may handle an ore train to Atikokan and a time freight back to Port Arthur.

When a loaded train is ready at Atikokan, a crew is called and an extra train is ordered east to run to Port Arthur. The train departs Atikokan and runs directly to Neebing Yard, west of Fort William. At Neebing Yard, the loaded ore cars are weighed and classified. After weighing and classification, the cars are stored at the Hillyard until the dock agent orders them to be spotted on the ore dock at Port Arthur.

Power for the ore dock assignments is varied. This writer has seen 3 switch engines MUed pushing ore cars onto the ore dock. Switch engines are also used as 2 unit combinations and single unit assignments, depending upon the work that has to be done. The maximum number of cars that is shoved onto the dock is 50 cars. The ore dock is 1200 feet long, and each track has a capacity of 50 cars just as the LS&I dock has in Marquette, Michigan.

The main line between Port Arthur and Atikokan is very modern in every respect. In order to handle the ore traffic, the line is either double track with movement by signal indication or single track with Centralized Traffic Control.

The future of the CN ore operations on the Steep Rock is very bright. A pellet plant was recently completed and the other ore deposits are very rich. American and Canadian Steel Companies have invested a considerable amount of money into the development of the Steep Rock, and are now looking forward to depending upon Steep Rock ore for many decades.

Recently, the Canadian National has completed construction of a 67 mile branch line to a new mine site at Bruce Lake, Ontario. The new line runs north from the transcontinental main line at Amesdale, Ontario to Bruce Lake. Production at this new mine and pellet plant began in mid-1968. The ore trains roll from Bruce Lake to Amesdale, then east on the main line to Superior Junction, and then south on the Graham Subdivision to Port Arthur, a distance of approximately 253.5 miles. This is the longest iron ore run anywhere in the Lake Superior Region. At the lake port, the iron ore pellets are handled through a new loading and storage facility built at the Valley Camp Coal Company dock. With this new development and the Steep Rock Range expansions, the iron ore railroading of the Canadian National will be around for a long time to come.

The Reserve Mining Company Railroad

The Reserve Mining Company railroad is a 47 mile line between Babbitt, Minnesota and Silver Bay on Lake Superior. Reserve's railroad, like Eries's, is not a common carrier. Its sole function is the hauling of raw taconite ore.

The Reserve's taconite pellet plant is located at Silver Bay; the taconite mine is at Babbit. Reserve is the only company that does not operate a pellet processing plant on the Mesabi Range, as do Erie, U. S. Steel and the M. A. Hanna Company. Therefore, Reserve must haul its crude taconite to the Lake Superior port for processing and shipping. The Company's Silver Bay plant produces about 10.7 million tons of

AN ORE TRAIN preparing to leave a mine at Atikokan, Ontario.—*Courtesy CNR*

A VIEW of the ore dock approach with a train.—*Courtesy CNR*

pellets per year. For this production of high grade iron ore pellets, the railroad carries about 31 million tons of crude ore from the Babbitt mine per year. This means that the Reserve Mining Company railroad ranks as one of the top three ore haulers in the entire United States. The other two roads are the DM&IR and the Penn Central. As of this writing, the Reserve is slightly ahead of the DM&IR and the Penn Central.

The Reserve Mining Company railroad is one of the most modern in the World. The road itself is double track and built with 140 pound welded steel rail. This is the heaviest rail made today. The railroad is also equipped with centralized traffic control.

In order to handle the 31 million tons annually, Reserve operates 17 road locomotives of 1750 horsepower each, type SD-9 and four switch engines, two 800 horsepower and two 1200 horsepower and 990 ore cars. The ore cars

are about 30 feet long and are the only flat bottom type ore cars used anywhere in the Lake Superior Region.

The ore cars are loaded at the Babbitt mine with ore that has been crushed to minus three-inch chunks. Each car has a capacity of 85 long tons.

After about 160 cars have been loaded, a Babbitt Division crew takes the train on the three hour run to Silver Bay. Upon arrival, the road crew yards its train and receives orders for taking an empty train back to Babbit. Reserve and Erie are the only two campanies in the Lake Superior Region that operate their ore crews in a turn around run from the Range to Lake Superior and return. All other lines, except the Canadian National operate from the Lake to the Range and return.

After the ore cars have been yarded at Silver Bay, a switch engine readies the train for dumping by two rotary car dumpers. The cars are spotted two at a time automatically, rolled over without uncoupling from each other or the rest of the train and return to the level position in about 90 seconds.

The ore cars are equipped with specially designed swivel couplings which permit dumping without uncoupling—a truly remarkable operation.

With an average of 9 ore trains per day, the Reserve line is one of the busiest railroads in the Lake Superior Region. It truly can be called a little giant in view of its heavy trains, double track and CTC. The management of Reserve Mining Company is to be commended for its outstanding job of ore hauling.

The Erie Mining Company Railroad

The responsibility of the Erie Mining Company Railroad is the hauling of taconite pellets from the company's plant at Hoyt Lakes to Taconite Harbor. The railroad is 72 miles long and is single track. There are spur sidings at

approximate 14 mile intervals and a main passing siding near the midpoint.

The trains are loaded at two areas at the Hoyt Lakes Plant. Current production pellets are loaded directly into the cars by an automatic loading pocket. Blocks of 12 cars are moved under the pocket through the use of a trackmobile. At the same time another string of ore cars are being loaded by stock pile shovel from the pellets that were produced during the winter. A switch engine handles these cars and generally has time to make up the entire train for the main line units.

In order to ship the production of 7½ million tons of pellets per year, the Erie dispatches four trains per day to Taconite Harbor. The crews are called at Hoyt Lakes when a loaded train is ready. The main line power usually consists of 5 F-9's, and each train is usually about 120 cars. The running time for the trains from Hoyt Lakes to Taconite Harbor is about 3 hours.

A VIEW of the CNR ore dock at Port Arthur.—*Courtesy CNR*

Upon arrival at Taconite Harbor, the train, normally containing 10,000 net tons of pellets, is dumped in about 6 to 7 minutes while in motion at speeds up to 10 miles per hour. This is accomplished by contact between a dumping device on each ore car and ramp rails which extend the full length of the dock.

The dumping device consists of an automobile tire and wheel mounted on each side of the car. The wheel is attached to dumping gear on the car so that revolution in a clockwise direction will open the car doors. The closing of the doors is accomplished in like manner by the wheel on the opposite side of the car, when it contacts a raised rail at the west end of the ore dock.

After the train is completely empty, it returns to Hoyt Lakes taking about 2 hours to makes the return trip. Trains are handled by 3 man crews.

The Ore Dock

The Erie Mining Company dock at Taconite Harbor is 1200 feet long with a storage capacity of 110,000 tons of pellets. The dock contains 25 pellet storage bins at 48 foot centers. Each bin is serviced by a retractable conveyor to transfer the pellets to the ore boats. Each belt can load in excess of 1500 tons per hour.

The **Erie Mining** Company Railroad was built in 1954. It is the newest ore hauler in the Lake Superior Region. The railroad and the ore dock are without doubt, one of the most efficient bulk handling transportations systems found anywhere in the world.

The Algoma Central Railroad

There is one other railroad that handles iron ore products to a Lake Superior Port. That line is the Algoma Central. In this case, the railroad handles iron ore from Wawa to Michipicoten, a distance of about 9 miles. At Michipicoten, the railroad maintains an ore dock with 2200 ton per hour belt conveyor loading system. The storage capacity of the dock is 20,000 tons and it was built in 1939.

The tonnage through Michipicoten is rather small compared to the other ore carriers. However, most of the ore mined in the Wawa area is carried by an all rail route to the steel mills at Sault Ste. Marie, Ontario. The total annual tonnage for the ACR amounts to around 3 million tons. The traffic is carried in standard 34 foot hopper cars with a 140,000 pound capacity.

ERIE MINING COMPANY'S taconite pellet loading dock at Taconite Harbor, Minnesota, is located 81 miles from Duluth on the north shore of Lake Superior. Pellets are transported from the taconite plant, 74 miles inland, in 96 car trains. Cars are unloaded automatically as the train moves over the dock. Erie Mining Company is managed by Pickands Mather & Co.

HERE IS A VIEW of two reserve SD-9's during construction of the Silver Bay plant and dock.—
Courtesy Reserve Mining Co.

THE CANADIAN NATIONAL has two basic types of ore cars: 62½ ton capacity and 82½ ton capacity. These cars were built by National Steel Car Corp. at Hamilton, Ontario.—*Courtesy National Steel Car Corp.*

IN 1966 WHEN PELLETS began their flow on the Canadian National, the road took several of the 82½ ton cars and added extensions to them.—*Courtesy Canadian National Ry.*

AFTER THE TRAINS are loaded at Babbitt they are hauled to Silver Bay by 4 SD-9's. The trains, approximately 9 per day, run all winter long as this photo shows.— *Courtesy Reserve Mining Company*

THIS IS THE TYPE of ore car that is used to haul pellets from the Hoyt Lakes plant to dock at Taconite Harbor on the Erie Mining Company Railroad.—*Courtesy Bethlehem Steel Co.*

A RESERVE MINING COMPANY railroad ore train being loaded with raw taconite ore at the Babbit, Minnesota mine.—*Courtesy Reserve Mining Company*

UPON ARRIVAL AT SILVER BAY, the train is yarded. Later a switch engine moves the cars through the car dumper, which empties the cars two at a time.—*Courtesy Reserve Mining Company*

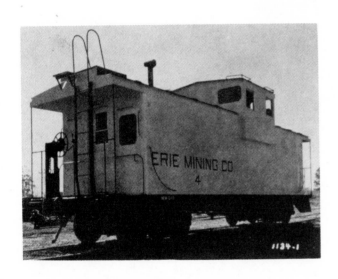

RECENTLY, EMC took delivery of several cabooses from International Car Corp. The company's original cabooses were bay window cars.—*Courtesy International Car Corp.*

A RESERVE MINING COMPANY caboose used on the road trains.—*Courtesy International Car Corp.*

INDEX

142

AN AERIAL VIEW of the ore classification yard at Escanaba. This yard will be retired upon completion of the new ore dock and train yard in 1969.